EXPERIMENTS IN AQUARIAN MAGIC

A practical handbook of occult techniques for the Aquarian
Age.

EXPERIMENTS IN AQUARIAN MAGIC

A guide to the magical arts and skills that will
unlock the secrets of the 'Gods for the Future'.

by

MARIAN GREEN

THE AQUARIAN PRESS
Wellingborough, Northamptonshire

First published 1985

© MARIAN GREEN 1985

British Library Cataloguing in Publication Data

Green, Marian
    Experiments in aquarian magic: a guide to the
    magical arts and skills that will unlock the
    secrets of the 'gods for the future'.
    1. Magic
    I. Title
    133.4'3   BF1611

    ISBN 0-85030-407-5

The Aquarian Press is part of the Thorsons Publishing Group

Printed and Bound in Great Britain by
Whitstable Litho Ltd., Whitstable, Kent

CONTENTS

Dedicated to all my friends on
the Paths of Magic.

INTRODUCTION

Magic still holds its ancient enchantment. Although we find ourselves living in a technological civilization, at the end of the twentieth century, the fascination for things hidden, occult knowledge and the workings of esoteric societies still draws many of us to the doorway to the Mysteries.

This book is an attempt to explain some of the many arts whose roots are lost in the distant past, yet whose fruits and flowers may still be gathered in this modern age. We now have the language of psychology to give us contemporary terms for what our ancestors spoke of as 'supernatural'. We have electronic equipment which can measure, assess and store information which magicians in the past could only know by intuition, and retain in memory. We talk about 'altered states of consciousness' whilst the priests of the past knew of visions and oracular messages. We discover answers in books, and stored on tape and computer discs. Long ago, when it was believed that writing down secret knowledge profaned it, the magicians relied on their own memories, on nature and the tides of the world to remind them of their sources of wisdom and inspiration.

Even now, to walk the paths of magic involves taking a journey into an unseen and largely unmapped domain. Much of it is within the mind and consciousness of every individual practitioner. It is possible to be guided by signposts, be directed by those who have made similar journeys, but really every assay into the realms of the occult is an adventure, or as expressed in the title of this book, an experiment. Like laboratory experiments it is necessary to gather equipment, keep a log-book or journal, plan each stage of the work and dress in clothes suitable for the job in hand. You will need to cleanse yourself, the physical space for these experiments, and the 'psychic' area, as well. Just as the bacteriologist has to be very careful about contamination affecting his work, so must the magician leave outside all disruptive feelings; he must avoid disturbances, and achieve a complete focus of attention on the object of his ritual or meditation. In both cases the more familiar you become with the techniques of the experiments the more reliable the results will be.

Magic is not for the faint-hearted, nor is it a subject which can be tackled entirely from your armchair. Just as with any other subject you will only succeed in working your magical will if you dedicate yourself wholeheartedly to the process. You cannot dabble and expect to get safe or satisfactory results from desultory acts. You must be prepared to commit your time, your energy and your resources (not necessarily money) to the study, practice and mastery of a wide variety of skills. You will need to examine closely your beliefs in your own abilities, in the concept of God or the Gods and Goddesses of modern pagan religions. You will need to persist, to work with patience and perseverence even if nothing seems to be happening.

As you will realize, magic does not necessarily work to satisfy greed, nor to give you power, nor to solve all the little difficulties encountered in the modern world. You won't become rich overnight, nor will all your feelings of insecurity or inferiority vanish in a puff of incense smoke! To obtain results you will have to WORK VERY HARD, commit yourself to continuous effort, perhaps for months or years, and always strive to become a better, more effective human being.

The ultimate aim of all magical work is SERVICE. We may use the ancient arts to heal, to disclose aspects of the future, to become wiser, not purely for our own benefit, but because that is part of the purpose of our existence on Earth. Any traditional school of magic will make this very plain to students, and so will reputable books on the subject. You must be prepared to have your life shaped by the kind of magic you intend to use. If you join a coven and devote your work to knowing the Goddess and the God as they manifest through the festivals of the year, or you work Natural Magic (healing with herbs, divining with twigs, cherishing the Earth), you will follow a different path to those who seek knowledge of the inner Temples and the rites of High Magic. In either case (or in any other you may discover on your journey through the Mysteries), you will be directed so that the Great Work may be accomplished. You may meet people seemingly by coincidence; you may read books by chance, or from your own inner resources discover the precise key which fits the door to your next stage of unfoldment. Things will certainly happen to you if you dare to take up the challenge of Aquarian Magic – they always have! But that is part of the adventure of magic. Remember these techniques ARE EXPERIMENTS – *you* are the guinea pig, and your results may not be the same as those of any other practitioner. TAKE CARE, ACT SENSIBLY and WORK PATIENTLY through these different experiments in Aquarian Magic.

In *Magic for the Aquarian Age* some of the most important techniques were spelled out, whilst other areas were passed over in a more superficial manner. In this book, less attention will be given to detailing topics. Here sufficient information is given for students to make their own tests and trials of a wide variety of different subjects. If you find ideas here which you have never seen dealt with in the context of magic, or if the path which led you towards the occult way has come via some other field of knowledge not covered here, this book will help to open new doors to understanding and interest.

There are many aspects of modern occult work which some magicians or witches or other practitioners may not yet have attempted but now at the beginning of the Age of Aquarius, their knowledge should be expanded to cover a wider field than ever before.

One of the mainstays of effective magic is balance. The magician needs to balance the powers of change invoked by his rituals with his human skills and strengths. He or she needs to balance the inner forces with their outer understanding: the power of sun with the power of moon, the energy for growth with that for decay; justice with mercy, and equally important, male with female. Many people have stepped upon the path of the Mysteries because it seemed to lead away from the imperfect balance of patriarchy. They became pagans and worshipped the power of the Earth Mother and the Moon Goddess. The Aquarian magician, whether male or female, will need to explore both aspects within his/her inner nature and outer physical form and bring them into perfect harmony. Returning to the arms of the Mother is no better an idea than forever seeking the protection of the Father. We are all children of the Universe, just as we all have physical mothers and fathers. The Aquarian mage will seek the middle way, acknowledging Mother and Father, God and Goddess, Sun and Moon, not only without, but within his/her inner being too.

The experiments set out here are safe for anyone with a degree of common sense to try. Follow the instructions carefully, just as you would those on a packet of cake mix or for a new electronic gadget. If you feel you are getting out of your depth, or losing control, place your hand upon the floor, and 'earth' the power. If you design a pentacle and place it before you whilst you are working, it will have the same effect. Work at a steady pace through the different experiments, allowing time for each to work before going on to the next. Keep detailed notes, recording time, place, people and intention clearly – only then can you look back to assess your results. Enjoy this study, treat it seriously, make an effort to do the best you can in everything you attempt, and discover the excitement of achieving magical success.

1.
OPENING THE DOORS TO YOUR INNER MIND

Successful magic is the result of control on the part of the magician. If you set out casually to try some technique, forget some of the vital equipment, hear the telephone ringing in the middle and have no definite plan or purpose you are hardly likely to be successful, whether you are trying magic or biochemistry. If you are new to the subject, decide on an easily achievable goal for your first attempts at occult work. To hasten slowly in these ancient arts is never a waste of time. Make things as easy for yourself as you can. Cut down distractions from the outside, such as noise, interruptions, or anything else which might prevent you from relaxing, or carrying out your intentions.

Meditation

The first technique with which you ought to become very familiar is meditation. It permits you to 'switch off the world' and opens up the door to your memory, subconsciousness and what Dr Jung defined as the 'collective unconscious'. It doesn't matter if you don't fully understand these terms at present, as long as you are willing to take the view that there are areas of your personal memory, for example, which you cannot get at immediately. Can you recall the presents you were given for your sixth birthday? No? Well, somewhere in the depths of your memory that information is stored. Jung was convinced that as well as our personal memories we are able to delve into the memories of other people, either individuals, or even whole countries. It is where myths and ancient legends, shared by widely separated people, seem to have their roots. Anyone can learn to enter a relaxed state when the gates between the normal, waking, conscious mind and the inner self, collective unconscious, personal subconscious or Akashic Records (to use an occult term), may be gently caused to open. It requires a little patience, perseverance and a relaxed 'let's give it a try' attitude. You cannot force open these gates by will or by gritting your teeth, but by cunning and delicate pressure!

Find a time and place where you won't be disturbed for at least half an hour. You will need an upright chair and a notebook and pen for keeping a record (unless you already have a large 'magical' diary in which you enter dreams, books you have read, and any other magical work you are trying). Sit upright with your feet flat on the floor or on a thick book, and your hands resting comfortably on your lap. Breathe out fully, and then counting at your own speed, breathe in for a count of four. Hold your breath for four, breathe out for four, hold your breath out for another count of four, and then repeat the entire cycle six times. You may find this pattern difficult, in which case you can try 4-2-4-2, or even 8-4-8-4. You can count quickly or slowly, or if you can feel it without strain or ceasing to sit in a relaxed position, use your own pulse beat, felt in your wrist or neck. Focus your whole attention on counting and breathing comfortably. Gradually you will find this helps you to relax and bring your attention to the subject of the meditation. This may be a word, a name, a phrase from a book or poem, or a concept like 'peace in the world'.

Meditation is a knack, like balancing on a bicycle or swimming. Once you can do it, practice brings you greater rewards and longer periods of concentration. Don't try TOO HARD. Relax, and suddenly you will find words, images, still pictures or actions flitting past your point of awareness. Try to watch without attempting to grab hold of this material. Gradually you will find the film show slows down, or the images or non-visual concepts remain in your mind long enough for you to study them. Like remembering dreams, you may need to tell yourself what is happening to fix it in longer term memory.

Recent brainwave studies have shown that meditation tends to bring the patterns of brainwaves in each hemisphere of the brain into harmony. Many of the tasks of modern living, like language, mathematical logic and the written word seem to be dealt with in the left hemisphere, whilst imagination, pictures, spacial judgements and less 'logical' matters occur mainly in the right half. Any technique which brings about a better degree of balance between both halves, and allows more faculties to be used on any activity will help to balance the whole individual. Other studies have shown that intuition may be a cross-brain form of communication. (Some arts are performed with the left hand by right-handed magicians, because information such as that obtained with a dowsing pendulum can be processed more subtly by the right half of the brain.) When you begin to meditate you may almost feel the links within your brain being formed, or channels of information reopening – it's a weird sensation!

You can choose pictures, symbols, words or sentences taken from a book as subjects for meditation, but don't give up if nothing much happens the first few times. Sometimes it will take three or more sessions of about ten minutes each before you get the flow of information to start. It does get easier with regular practice. If you feel very tense or embarrassed at first you can jog on the spot or do any sort of stretching and bending exercises for a few minutes. Try to gently extend your spine, chest and shoulders for these can limit your ease of breathing, and many tense people find areas of stiffness in the neck, shoulders and upper back. Dancing to lively music where you move your whole body is good too, and the rhythms can help you get away from the stresses of everyday life.

Meditation early in the morning is generally better than sessions late at night, but if you have time during the day a quarter of an hour of relaxation and study can be extremely beneficial. Whatever you do, don't merely slump into bed and expect to receive revelations as you nod off. All these experiments need to be performed under proper controlled conditions – even those as basic as this! Your results will only become reliable if you persist with regular experiments.

Visualization

Another key method used by all magicians and witches is the art of creative visualization. Whereas meditation makes you the receiver of the 'programme' as it were, visualization puts you into the film-maker's chair. With your *imagi*nation, the most valuable tool of any *magi*cian, you can shape the future. You can find lost objects by seeing, in your inner mind, their location; or heal, by creating a picture of the sick person in full and happy health. You can build up an entire world as do many writers of science fiction, or painters of inspired pictures. You may create a magical Temple, a sacred sanctuary or even discover a guide to lead you through the doors of inner reality.

Like meditation, you need to relax, to calm your body and direct your attention by breathing in a regular, steady pattern for a few minutes. With your eyes closed place the image of a familar object in view. Some people can't 'see' this object, but you should be able to sense it, or imagine what it looks like by describing it in words. For example, say you choose a blue vase – either you see a 3-D solid image of the pot, or you see a vague, bluish item, changing shape and 'real-ness', or you get words like 'round', 'powder-blue', 'china', 'flowerpot', 'shiny', 'hard', 'symmetrical' and so on. You may feel the coolness of the china, or sense it solidity and stability. Different people get impressions in a variety of ways, but seeing a really solid picture is most helpful. Try objects which you know well, from ornaments to whole rooms, and DO CHECK YOUR OBSERVATIONS. When you begin to look into the future, details could be very important – so could those from the past.

If you visit ancient sites, or sacred places, try to focus these images for later recall. Take photographs or slides, if you can, to remind you of the real monument, the texture of building materials, the local plants and trees, the weather or temperature of the place and the entire ambience. Study illustrated books or films of places like the Temples of Ancient Egypt or Greece, sacred groves and stone circles or earthworks. Absorb all you can about the atmosphere and the patterns they make against the sky. If you are drawn to a particular place or period of history soak up all the data you can because, if later on you wish to create your own modern version of the place as a Temple or personal shrine, you will have the information already in your memory.

Once you get into the swing of using your imagination to create new scenes you might like to experiment with some of the more specifically magical techniques. The first is a circle of protection. There are lots of books on elaborate ways of performing the Lesser Banishing Ritual of the Pentagram and so on, but basically you only need to see yourself within a circle of bluish-white light to achieve the same effect nowadays. Sit on your chair and place, in your mind's eye, a ball of glowing fire about 3 feet (1 metre) from your feet; see it spinning and glowing strongly. As it whirls within itself it begins to rise off the ground. It swings outwards to the right trailing a comet-like tail of vivid light. Slowly you will find it makes a complete circle, rising above your head, then returning to the ground. You will now find that you can draw the entire circle towards you so that it goes below your feet and above your head. Once you get it there you can get it to turn over as if it was pivoted at about your hip level. It will swing round like a hoop, enclosing you in a sphere of brilliant, protective light. You can try the same experiment whilst standing up but remember, if you are relaxed, not to fall over when the light starts to swing end over end! It may take a few sessions of practice to get the clear feeling or vision of the circle being formed and then turning. When it has completed the circle the bright line will vanish, but a dimmer glow around you will remain. If you do this at least once each day, gradually it will strengthen your own aura.

The aim of such an exercise is to disinfect the area around you when you are meditating, or later performing magical work. Stray thoughts, worries or left-over problems will be kept at bay by this technique, so that what you perceive will be a clear vision, not scraps distorted by mundane matters. Just as the surgeon or chemist sterilizes his equipment and laboratory, so do magicians purify their immediate surroundings. You will be more aware after your sessions of meditation or visualization and so more sensitive to the feelings of others, or to the atmosphere of your home, etc. This will help you get over the 'culture shock' of new, wider perceptions, which could otherwise be a bit unsettling. Remember to reverse the process at the end of a session to 'switch it off'.

Some simple tests of your ability to visualize properly can be tried out, when you have a few days with plenty of time to spare. Each needs to be repeated several times. First, imagine a person you know well standing before you. Look at the image. Is it correct, does it capture their personality? Can you change the colour of their hair, their eyes? Make them taller or fatter? If you can, your imagination is playing tricks – because you have an image of a *real* person in front of you! You will need to bear this in mind if you start to explore your past lives, for example, because if you can 'bend' real people like that, what can you do about your supposed past?

Some Experiments in Creative Visualization

Sit down, perform your breathing patterns until you feel calm, then close your eyes. Imagine in front of you there is a large book. See its cover, examine the binding, the size, the thickness of it. Study every detail, and see if you can read its title. Reach out, in your mind, and feel it, smell it, caress the edges of the pages, the firmness of the spine, the hardness of the corners. Apply every one of your senses to this great book. (You may find this is a sufficient experiment on its own at first as it is a difficult skill for some people.)

In the next few sessions, open the book, study the printing or writing within. What can you read? Even if you only get glimpses, or if because you can't actually 'see' you sense the pages, try to imagine what could be written there. In any case, please note in your diary what you sensed each time. If nothing seems to work, try a different experiment, but do come back to this, for it could be the book of your life – or the future history of the world, made ready for you to read!

In another experiment (again to be carried out over a period of about a week, with one attempt each day), try to create the picture of a seed. See it in your hand, tiny but full of potential. In your mind plant it and over the next few days discover how it grows, what its leaves are like, the colour and shape of its flowers, their scent. Gradually allow it to develop, spreading branches, blossoming and growing taller. Watch it being pollinated, and see the fruits begin to form and ripen. Feel them, pick one and taste it. Describe every stage of the plant's development in your notes. Compare it with your own life – where are you? Just a sprig? In blossom or ready to cast off your leaves or your ripened fruit? Think about it.

Another week of creative visualization can be concerned with a fire. See, in your mind's eye, a tiny spark struck from flint and iron, set alight a tuft of tinder. Let that minute flamelet attack a twig, and gradually take hold on some dry sticks. Watch it burn through several sessions. Mentally pile on some green wood and watch the smoke, smell the steam and woodsmoke, feel the heat of the flames, hear the crackling twigs. See it send sparks and smoke upwards from its glowing base. Discover within the dying embers a cave of wonder and imagination. Find the mystery at the centre of the 'need' fire, the oracular hearth. Keep accurate notes of what you discover and perceive.

An exercise in which you awaken your ability to create within your mind's eye is the way you can offer service to others. I expect that if you think back through your life you will recall someone to whom you owe a debt; maybe it is money, maybe some good turn you never paid back. To exercise this new faculty, try to imagine a situation where you repay your debt to your friend. Again don't rush. Set it up as a problem and seek a real solution. Obviously your friend may be someone with whom you have lost touch, or may even date back to your school-days, so that an actual repayment of the debt is not possible. Set up a visualized situation in which a way is found to help or bring luck to that person. Imagine him or her getting an unexpected gift, which somehow repays what you owe. If you can begin this particular experiment in a waxing moon, it will make it more effective. Focus on the debt being repaid – then after about seven attempts, forget about it. You will eventually get to know what happened.

If you are owed a debt by someone else, or need a small favour or bit of luck, AFTER YOU HAVE ASTRALLY PAID YOUR DEBT, you may have a go at psychic debt-collecting. If a particular person owes you something, you don't necessarily have to collect from them. Ideally, as this work is using the magical forces of the universe (which can redistribute the finances etc., more fairly than mere humans would do), allow these forces to decide how your debt is to be repaid. Simply imagine the cash clearly, in crisp new notes, or in whatever form it is needed, landing on your doormat. Please note – angels, in the twentieth century, do not turn up with gold bricks at the whim of amateur magicians. Focus on the required thing arriving in an ordinary way for about seven sessions. Strangely, this can work quite well in a waning moon. It is usually more effective if you have a real need for something other than actual cash. A present, a holiday, some clothes and so on can all turn up as a result of this technique – but remember NEED not GREED will get the best results.

Energy Raising Methods

Sometimes meditation can leave you feeling a bit sleepy, or you may feel too tired to cope with something as relaxing as your regular visualization exercises. If you are physically tired and have things to do this method will work well too. In fact, if you go outside and lean on a big tree, you can get even faster and more active responses. To try this with a real tree, remove your shoes and stand with your back against the trunk of a large, healthy-looking tree. Lean back and close your eyes. You will begin best by imagining the life force from the earth being slowly drawn in through the roots of the tree, which spread out as far below you as do the branches above. You may visualize this as a dark greenish current, flowing steadily, slowly but extremely powerfully upwards, taking with it the essence of the Earth, the blood of Mother Nature. Just as it is drawn up within the trunk behind you, you will begin to sense a similar cool, strong flow rising upwards through your feet, gradually filling you with calmness and helping your spine to straighten and feel relaxed and stronger. If you can clasp your hands to the tree behind you, or above your head you will allow the flow of life force to go through you and return to the tree. Take your time over this.

When you have the Earth-force working steadily upwards

through you, you can begin to focus your attention on the down pouring Sky or Sun power. Whereas the Earth's energy is slow and steady and dark, the Sky power is bright, sparkling and darting. If you can imagine something like the sparks given off by a firework, silvery-gold fizzing down from the sky, entering every leaf and twig and sizzling downwards into your body, that is a way to experience it. Imagine a rain of light pattering upon the canopy of leaves above your head, and this sparkling energy gradually seeping down into your fingers and arms, your head and body, right down into your feet. It is the healing power of life and light, and is quite different from the steady, seeping Earth power. Feel the warmth of sunlight, the gentle play of a breeze, the effect of a spring shower on a thirsty tree, refreshing the leaves, and running into your veins to awaken sluggish thoughts, weary bones and stiff muscles. Allow your body to relax and revel for a while in the sprinkling downflow of Sky energy.

After a while, when you have fully appreciated the upthrusting Earth force, and the sparkling energy of the Sun and Sky separately, perform the harder task of feeling both at once. This may take a little practice. As the two energies are so different you ought to be able to sense them together. It is hard to explain the sensation, as everyone may feel a different version of it, but it is an extremely pleasant, refreshing and calming experience, and well worth doing a number of times. You may find that each variety of tree has its own way of transmuting the Earth and Sky forces. Oaks are slow-growing, immensely strong trees whilst beeches are more delicate. Birches seem to dance beneath the sky; willows may feel sad, though they are healing trees. Yews offer the dark wisdom of the Lady of the Waning Moon, and ashes the direct might of a King on his throne. The rowan will protect you from harm, and if you experiment with the trunk of an apple tree you may find you can enter the world of the Unseen, for it is the tree of the Silver Branch, which is the key to the Celtic otherworld. Although this may seem like natural magic rather than a ritual method, it is well worth trying out, with an actual tree. Once you have perceived these energy flows in the wild, you will be

able to bring the same exercise into the Temple, and
receive the same sort of effects.

Indoors, stand with bare feet and comfortable clothing,
facing east (or which ever direction you have decided is
ritually east), and begin to sense and see the up-welling
dark Earth power. Concentrate on this for at least a
minute, until you feel calm, strong and balanced. Then
begin to feel the descent of the sparkling bright Sun
power, invigorating and energizing, helping you to switch
into a higher gear for magical work, be it merely a
meditation, or an elaborate ceremony.

If you wish to turn this into the first part of a ritual, you
may say the following words (or make up some to suit
your beliefs or ideas, adding God or Goddess names,
angels or what ever seems most appropriate).

> From beneath me arises the energy of the Earth, my home
>   and my foundation,
> From above me pours down the Power of the Light of the
>   Sun and the enchanting Moon,
> To my Right hand flows the strength to control and direct,
>   the power of magic,
> To my Left hand comes the skill to divine and to heal, the
>   source of blessing.
> Before me arises the perfected one I strive to become, my
>   magical true self.
> Behind me falls the one I was, and with it, all my discarded
>   failures.
> Around me circle the eternal stars, lamps of wisdom in the
>   deeps of space.
> Within me grows the flame of life, the light of experience
>   and understanding.

This is a very powerful invocation which should be said
very slowly, allowing the full meaning of the words to
become apparent to you. Imagine the various forces
flowing to you. See clearly or imagine your perfected self,
your balanced magical personality standing in front of
you. Sense all your faults and failures being gradually cast
off, like a snake shedding its skin, curling and crumpling
down into ashes behind you. Try hard to overcome any
faults you have, deliberately setting them behind you.

You may observe that this prayer or invocation has

similarities to those found in other books you may have read. This is a new version for students working towards the new age, but you will find it as powerful and effective as that used in the past. Done with intent you will find it will completely clear the atmosphere for ritual, especially if you don't have a room which can be set aside purely for occult work. This invocation should be repeated at the conclusion of any work, and then you should firmly stamp your right foot twice, to complete the ceremony or meditation, and so on.

If you have difficulty sleeping, or are worried or disturbed you can imagine the circle which forms a ball around you, as described above, but see it as a glowing blue sphere. It will become an egg shape if you are standing up, and after a few moments it will shrink and become invisible but will act as a shield from distractions so that you can sleep, or perhaps feel safer in an unfamiliar atmosphere. Sometimes if you are travelling, or among strangers, or in some other sort of crowd whose pressure is uncomfortable, you can use it. This should only be a *temporary* form of protection, for the competent magician will be able to cope with alien atmospheres or a crowd of strange auras without becoming upset.

Although these basic exercises may be familiar to you from other books you have read, unless you have genuinely tried to master them, then none of the later experiments in this book will work so well for you. To be unable to switch off the world and enter a relaxed and receptive meditative state, or to be unable to picture clearly in your mind's eye or imagine and sense in some other way the surroundings for a ritual, a lost item or the recovery of a sick friend, then you will have a difficult task getting your magic to work. If it takes you months to perfect these methods not a moment of that time will have been wasted.

2.
JOURNEYS TO VISION

The Aquarian magician may be either a man or a woman, but there are many esoteric skills and arts which are much easier if you have a partner to help you. A lot has been written about 'soul-mates', 'twin-spirits' or 'magical partners' but much of it has misunderstood the true magical partnership. In the distant past the schools of magic trained young men and women each to fulfil particular esoteric roles. In the last century there were quite a few magical lodges where the select few contacted angelic forces, worked powerful rituals and progressed through a number of degrees, just as many of them still do. Like the patterns of everyday life, those which direct the magical work for the new age are also changing. Instead of working in huge factories, each being a little cog in a large wheel, more and more people are working alone, in small concerns, or for larger enterprises, but instead of joining up in a vast building, they are linked via telephone or computer lines ot their own terminal. Read Alvin Toffler's *The Third Wave* for a detailed explanation of the changes that are affecting the world of work. A similar current is washing through the occult world too.

The Aquarian Magician
The magician of the Aquarian Age will be a balanced, competent individual who probably works with just one partner, or in a small group of less than ten people. He or she will be less concerned with passing through many degrees than with achieving a better understanding of the ways in which it is possible to serve the forces of magic, and the world in general. The underlying reason for

magical work has always been service, but it has often been overlooked by self-centred individuals whose striving for personal power and position has formed the theme for many occult novels. Some people still yearn for the ability to dominate, to control and to direct the wills of less secure individuals, but that is only a short-sighted and limited use of the real forces. The competent modern adept will have sought to perfect his own understanding of life, have sorted out his material situation and have gained a deep knowledge of his inner abilities. Any skills he needs will have been practised and refined. Any weaknesses in his character or situation will have been examined carefully, not hidden in the depths of his psyche to bother him later on. The way to recognize an adept is not by the collection of ankhs and pentagrams around his neck, nor the flowing black cloak he wears to esoteric fairs, but by the effective way he copes with crises, the control he has when provoked, the span of his knowledge and his sympathy towards other people. If you can't cope with the ordinary world, you can be certain that you won't manage the inner worlds!

Any exercise or experiment which helps you to understand yourself, which bridges the gap between inner awareness and the 'real' world, such as meditation on your name, horoscope or ambitions, will all help you to be able to assess the needs of others, and so help them. Certainly, sitting alone, or with a friend, listening to quiet music and trying to understand where you want to go in life doesn't sound half as exciting as intoning sonorous words in a forgotten tongue, in an elaborate Temple thick with incense smoke, whilst wearing fabulous robes – but it is a lot safer, and is likely, in the long run, to be more effective! Later on, when you have an idea of where you want to go can you begin to collect all the paraphernalia, make the robes and regalia, construct, dedicate and make use of the Temple. To begin with you will need to open gently a few locked doors inside your mind, and explore some of the nooks and crannies of you own experiences before doing anything more exotic.

Magic tends to produce quite an number of 'Which comes first?' syndromes. If you want to meditate you may have been told that you need to consecrate the room first, and to consecrate a place you will need certain equipment, which also needs to be cleansed and dedicated before use and maybe you don't have the finances to purchase the things needed for this elaborate process. If you use the simple invocation in the last chapter, seeing or imagining clearly each part, this gets over the 'bless-the-items-to-dedicate-the-objects-to-consecrate-the-room-with' problem! You will be using the ultimate instrument of Aquarian Magic, that is, the trained human mind. Later on you can get on with the consecrations and rituals when you can imagine the ideal setting, and have sufficient confidence and experience to make them work.

Meditate on your own name, on the body you have (and look for ways of making this better, healthier and more skilled – no one else can do this for you!) and on your aims in life, both magical and mundane. If you can construct an image of how you would like to be, and then compare it with what you are, noting the differences, you can gradually begin to change for the better. Without a concept of the ideal, you will have no form to use as a pattern. Only you can decide what your own criteria are, based on previous experiences, situations and expectations. Examine the people around you for someone who can share, equally, your attempts to master magic and gain wisdom and power. Ideally the mage of the Aquarian Age will be one of a pair or small group, of men and women, all striving to become whole.

Choosing a Partner

It is difficult trying to understand what sort of partnership this may be, especially if forming relationships is not one of your best skills. You will need to find a companion you can trust, and who will trust you. He or she will need to be a person with whom you get on well, and who can be relied on, just as you must also be totally reliable. You will need to become firm friends, but it doesn't imply you need to go to bed together, nor that you must live in each others' pockets. You will have to be patient and tolerant, and neither should dominate the partnership. Each will excel at certain things, whilst the other is only fairly good – each will need to discover and refine any inbuilt talents, be they for healing, for ritual, for organization or for specifying what sort of work you will do together. You will have to find ways of operating, in the words of the witch's rule 'In perfect love and perfect trust'. This is no easy undertaking, because each of you will have to give and take, to act unselfishly and with the common good always above your own needs. Don't rush into a partnership with the first half-interested individual you encounter. If you start to train your inner awareness it will help you find and recognize a companion on the path far more reliably than searching the small ads in the papers!

Pathworking

If you do find someone who is willing to work with you, then you can experiment with the ancient art of pathworking. This is the magical application of story telling, yet another aspect of creative visualization, and an important key to effective magic. You can manage alone, recording the words on a cassette tape, or by learning the stages and telling yourself, but it is much easier if you are with a friend or in a small group. You should take it in turn to read the narrative, or make up the details of the story or description, so that you each gain the confidence of speaking in a magical context, and of being able to imagine and invent the situation of a occult operation.

Originally the paths were those of the Qabalah's Tree of Life, and the images were specifically related to the colours, the angelic forces and the mystical symbols which were associated with each path which joins the spheres on the Tree. An excellent modern work is *The Shining Paths* by Dolores Ashcroft-Nowicki (Aquarian Press). Today, a wide variety of magical paths may be walked in the imagination, from the examination of a specific symbol to lengthy journeys through time and space. This is a very effective way of reaching the relaxed yet perceptive state required for magical work. You may find a selection of contemporary books which detail ways of travelling into the recesses of the mind by way of a trip to the seaside, by becoming an actor in a medieval legend, or by entering your own, ordinary familiar workplace or home, and interacting with your family, your boss and your colleagues in a new way. Paths to the contemporary world can be just as important and effective as those

which lead to the land of legend and the matter of myths!
You will need about half an hour when you won't be
disturbed, and either a companion or a tape recorder to
tell the story. If you wish to relax first, do a bit of bending
and stretching and perform the invocation which will
help clear the atmosphere and make the work easier. You
can light a candle and some incense, close the curtains
and change into a magical robe as well, if you feel this will
help you. If none of these things is important to you,
simply ensure you won't have to answer the phone or the
door, etc. Sit upright in your meditation chair and
breathe slowly for a while and then start the tape, or ask
your story-teller to begin. Your partner might say something like the following:

> You are standing on a path at the foot of a rocky hill. It is late
> afternoon on a warm summer's eve. You are alone. You can
> sense the rough track beneath your feet, hear the wind
> rustling the grass and bushes near the path, and feel the after-
> glow warmth of the setting sun. It is very quiet. Soon you
> begin to climb the path, following its twists and turns,
> climbing upwards all the time. You notice the colour of the
> rocks, and the small flowering plants that cling to crevices.
> You touch the stone as the path gets steeper, seeking
> handholds, feeling it rough and warm beneath your hands.
> Up and up you go, scrambling up a narrow crack where the
> tread of other climbers has worn a clear set of footholds.
> After a really steep bit, you find yourself on a small plateau,
> and as you begin to get your breath back you hear the sound
> of running water. At the back of the plateau is an abrupt cliff,
> and a tiny runnel of pure water flows from it, into natural
> smooth basin, carved out by time from the bare stone. Here
> you pause, washing your hot face and hands, drinking the
> chilly, fresh water. You feel refreshed and filled with a kind
> of blessing.
>   Looking about you you notice that the sun is about to set,
> and scarlet streamers of cloud seem to be on fire on the
> western horizon. It is like watching a great bonfire gradually
> cooling, with dark grey-blue smokey clouds rising out of the
> red-orange lit sky. Above the darker clouds the sky is still
> daylight pale, yet here and there the bright points of stars
> and planets glitter above you. For a long time you stand, just
> watching the fiery colours fade, the piled clouds darken and
> turn grey, the sky change from blue through greenish-grey

to indigo as the last rays of the sun fade below the horizon. It is very still, but you gradually notice a cool wind has sprung up, it puffs a sharp and chilling breeze on your face, and you turn your back to stop bits of grass blowing into your eyes. It gets stronger and almost pushes you towards the steep track where you came to the plateau. You find yourself gently shoved over the edge, down the smooth rocks, finding each hand and foot hold firm where you need it. Gradually the path becomes less difficult, levelling out as you reach the bottom of the hill. In the twilight you can still make out the plants and the white flowers which seem almost to glow in the fading eventide. Once you are certain you can go down no further you will find the image of the hillside fading. Slowly you sink back into your ordinary room and when you are ready your eyes open and you feel you have returned from a refreshing and relaxing journey.

Your companion should allow you plenty of time to breathe deeply a few times, and get up and stretch. You should write down the images, the impressions and feelings you received during your journey, as these tend to vanish like dreams do, unless recorded or thought through quickly.

This is a very simple experiment. You will both need to try out ways of reading the text, to get the speed and atmosphere right for you. If you wish to add recorded music or even sound effects like the sea, or the wind, or just use quiet background music to cut out the distraction of traffic or other disturbing noises, it will all help. This first path was just a trip through the elements, and if you examine your experience, you ought to be able to detect which was most real — the rock and path; the trickling spring; the fiery sunset and its warmth on your skin, or the cool breeze. Think back and reread your notes to discover which was the most potent, not just as a scene but as an experience. When your companion has also made this journey or a similar one, you can discover which sort of narrative is most helpful.

A pathworking is a way of exploring ancient sites, the Temples of Egypt, or the Tombs of Mycenae, by visiting them when they were new. We will come back to other applications of the art at a later stage. For now it is necessary to practise the technique of travelling, and of reading or making up a story or journey as you go along.

You will need to change gradually from the ordinary world into the visionary place and then return equally slowly and carefully. This is a very effective relaxation technique and it doesn't help to have the telephone ring in the middle, or someone come to the door. It won't do you much harm, having to leap up suddenly, but it makes it much harder to relax and tune in to the other scene the next time. Do your best to get rid of anything which might interfere, and ask your companion to deal with the unexpected.

This exercise is a good way of creating a calm feeling which will help you if you are using any form of divination. You can imagine yourselves going to the place of wisdom and understanding so that when you look at the Tarot cards, or throw the hexagrams of the *I Ching* you will see their message more clearly. If you have plenty of time to experiment, you can see each card of the Tarot trumps, for example, as the symbol on a door through which you pass to the world shown thereon.

Combining Divination and Pathworking

To combine the techniques of divination with path-working you could make a set of symbol cards showing a straight path, a crooked one, a field, a mountain, a valley, a well or spring, a sunset, a bonfire, clouds, a street, a cave, a forest, a glade, a chapel, an ancient monument, a castle, a garden, a stone circle, a gate, a coffer, some treasure, a magical object which is personal to you, and so on. You could cut out pictures from magazines if you can't draw (you would be surprised how many relevant images can be found in advertisements, holiday brochures and travel catalogues). Shuffle these pictures face down and then select about seven of them. Turn them over and then work out a narrative which takes you from your own home along a familiar road and out through a gate in a wall, or through the entrance to a building which you have never entered – you don't know for certain that it isn't the entrance to fairyland!

You can collect colours, images and relevant symbols and on a large diagram of the Tree of Life, or a magical journey, place the pieces to make a sensible transition from the base which is your home, or Malkuth on the

Tree, upwards on the journey. You can even devise a game, in which you have to collect items, colours, symbols or friends, rather in the way some of the computer or 'Dungeons and Dragons' games suggest, so that you can progress. Although this may seem a light-hearted way to approach something as serious as magical training, it is nevertheless a good way of becoming used to the images and patterns associated with whichever tradition you have chosen to study. You will allow this important material to sink into your memory and subconscious mind where it can work with your intuition, which you will also be training during such games, to produce clear and wide-ranging answers to divinations and meditations. You cannot expect to get out information or understanding if the raw material for it doesn't exist first, any more than you can learn to speak the words of another language without some sort of training. Put in plenty of data and your inner self and mind's eye can produce intricate and relevant answers and explanations. Experiment with simple methods until you can easily recall a range of 'correspondences'; symbols, colours, planetary information and God/Goddess names, etc., associated with any topic that comes into your head. It is the framework of many later magical operations, like making talismans, designing a personal sigil, visualizing the Temple of your dreams and so on.

With your magical companion do practise reading the answers to simple questions from your divining arts, wandering along the inner pathways and becoming used to the gentle transition to the meditation state with a friend in attendance. Play games with symbols, learn the basic skill of astrology and the images of the Tarot, always allowing your own intuition, rather than someone else's interpretation, to guide you.

You can design paths to strengthen your own or your companion's balance between the elements. Invent paths about the Earth, with fields, trees, caves, farmland and rocks if you feel 'out of this world' or if your charts show a lack of earth signs or planets in earth signs. Imagine every leaf on a tree, the development from a seed to a fruiting plant and so on. This is a slow session, gradual and powerful.

If your emotions give you trouble, work with Water, visualizing a spring welling from the hard rock, flowing gently into still lakes or imagine the pounding waves of the tide-surging ocean. Become part of that water, as gentle rain or storm-tossed waves; a trickling streamlet laughing over the waterfalls, or a slow-flowing broad river mouth, finding unity in the great sea. See cups and cauldrons, the banks of rivers and the cliffs by the beach and notice how they shape and control the water, changing and limiting it. Become a cup yourself, even the Holy Grail, when all your feelings are natural, when they find their own level and are not repressed, and you can respond honestly to all those around you.

When you feel weary and lacking in vitality, or your horoscope shows a deficit of Fire, then you will need to try the images of volcanoes, lightning, bonfires, furnaces, flames and lantern light. Feel the heat, smell burning incenses and see flowers glowing in bright sunlight. You should find this will raise your energy level, especially if you imagine the vitality and healing power of the sun, the darting light of flames and lightning flashing through you to awaken and add zest to your life.

If your mind is troubled and seems forever to be flitting from one subject to another so that you can't concentrate, look at the clouds. Watch from a high window, or lie down on your back in a garden, see how slowly clouds form and reform, change and merge, split and vanish. You can actually push them apart if you try, with a single large cloud. See a gap forming in the centre of a long cloud, and you will find it will begin to happen. Once the cloud has divided, you can cut up one half as it drifts lazily across the azure sky. It will take quite a few minutes of concentration to get this to happen, but it is a way of improving your attention span, and directing it towards Air, which is the mind element. For visualizations work with the effect the wind has on trees or fields of wheat. See mountain peaks, journeys by plane, birds winging free and safely through the sky; imagine flying with them on a homeward flight, above the houses of cities or the forests of the country. Become a kite safely anchored to earth, or a cloud shedding rain upon the waiting fields, a wind whistling through a rock, or a gentle breeze caressing the face of someone you love.

How to Awaken Your Senses

You can awaken your own senses by simple experiments. Close your eyes and examine the textures of things around you; the carpet, the edges of pages of a book, a wooden spoon or the petals of a flower. Touch them as gently as you can, not only with your fingertips, but with your cheek, your bare toes, your elbow. When you next eat a salad or a crisp apple, shut your eyes and savour every texture and sensation, not just the taste but the very feel of each bite. Play games with your companion, allowing him or her to feed you samples of things to recognize by taste or texture, letting you smell things without seeing them, or feel objects or materials hidden in a plastic sack or cardboard box. Find similar objects for your partner to examine with different senses to those normally used. It all helps you become aware of small clues, which can often be all you get during magical activities.

When you are divining you may only get a hint which flashes across your awareness very swiftly; or catch a glimpse of an image in a crystal; or smell a whiff of something during a ceremony; or feel a texture whilst travelling some distant path, and from that you will need to be able to detect a great deal. If you have a few moments to spare each day, do practise feeling, hearing, sensing, smelling and so on. I am sure you will remember instances when a trace of some long-forgotten scent awoke strong recollections of school, or your childhood, or a place you used to live in. The same can happen when you are delving through past lives or distant places.

Another valuable but frequently overlooked source of valuable material is literature. We have become so used to the written word that we forget it can provide valuable material to practise expanding our awareness with. Take any well written thriller, science fiction book or adventure novel and try to live through the character's experiences. You may well find the places described come swiftly before your inner eye, the excitement speeds up your heartbeat, the scenes encountered blot out your real surroundings. If you don't like fiction, there are plenty of excellent books on mountaineering, jungle explorations, adventures with unknown people, encounters with wild animals and so on, and even biographies of not very well-known people can produce episodes so vivid and exciting that you can share these experiences. They will never be the same as your own experiential material, but they do strengthen and test your abilities to enter into a rapt state when reality can be changed, and that after all, is a valuable asset in the magician's armory of practical skills.

Radio plays can expand your ability to 'see' in the mind's eye; descriptions in books can expand your awareness; using your fingers, your cheek, your nostrils or your tongue you can enter new worlds of sensation and experience. Though these ideas may be a long way from your original idea of magic this is simply because the world we are living in is changing rapidly, and senses like memory, taste and touch are being blunted by living in a world which does not need them for survival. In days before the majority of people could read everyone had to remember the names of things like trees, plants, animals and useful materials, whereas we look up the name of an unfamiliar plant, or the varieties of fungi which are safe to eat. Our world is cushioned and soft, not like the roughness encountered in the clothing, building materials and everyday items used by our ancestors even a hundred years ago. We recognize food from the packet or tin, or the writing on the wrapping, not by the scent or taste – with some things only the written information gives any clue as to what the foodstuff is!

You can write a short path to lead you to a pleasant place for your meditation – into a summer garden, to the side of a still lake, or a forest glade. Enter gently into this sanctuary away from the bustle of the everyday world and you will be surprised how much easier it is to unravel the subject of your meditation. In the clear air of the magical landscape images flow, ideas unroll and the most complex topic is sifted into more easily understood patterns. When you have made more progress in the magical arts this same technique can be used in many ways, one of which is the creation of a Temple of Wisdom, exactly tailored to your ideals and needs. Gradually its form will be shown to you and your companions. If you explore, discuss and shape it between you, it will become very 'real' within the magical context, and when you are ready to perform ceremonies, or enter into the deeper studies and thanksgivings or ritual workings you will have a home to go to which you can replicate in this ordinary world.

Scrying

Another basic experiment which you can try at this point is a version of scrying, the old name for crystal gazing. A sphere of polished rock crystal is a very expensive and rare item and it is not the easiest scrying glass for a beginner to learn with either. You can make a 'black mirror' quite simply, and the dark glass will tend to evoke clearer images for novices. Get a small round picture frame with its glass, either a piece of black velvet or a pot of matt black paint, and some silver paint, too. Take the glass out of the frame and paint one side with at least three coats of matt black paint, or place a circle of velvet cut to fit the frame under the glass. Meanwhile paint the frame itself silver – this is to link it with the 'psychic' energies of the Moon. When the paint is completely dry, make sure the unpainted side of the glass is outwards. Meditate, focus with a path to a place where a door to vision can be encountered, or simply light a candle and relax with a few cycles of the breathing pattern. Hold the black mirror where you can look into it without there being too many patches of light reflected in it. It should seem to be a deep pool of dark water. Allow your vision to go below the surface, and casually observe what you can see with your eyes focused within. Try to watch without tension and without worrying what you might see. Only by getting the balance of attention right will you see anything at all.

It is usual to find that the glass seems to cloud over, becoming dull as if mist had swirled across it. Usually you are so surprised by this that you lose the sensation. When this has become steady again you may find a sort of clearing within the smoky outline begins to form, and you seem to be absorbed into the dark centre. Here proper pictures, moving or still, black and white or coloured, scenes or symbols, numbers, words, shapes, people or action will be perceived. Different people will see a different version of this material. Some of it may be from the future, the past, or some other place. It can be like television, with short flashes of information or lengthy activities and events. You can feel as if you are a part of this, or merely an observer, unable to influence or participate. To get regular, clear images which make sense will take A LOT OF PRACTICE. You will need to make continued attempts for a long time before you have the skill to perceive consistently the future, events remote from you, or other material in which you are interested.

The curved glass from an old-fashioned alarm clock set into a round rim and backed with layers of black paint makes another good scrying glass, or even a thick disc of plate glass or perspex set into a frame of dull-coloured velvet or felt. Some people can manage with an ordinary glass mirror, a chunk of obsidian, black glass used on shop fronts or any other reflective material. Experiment! That is what it is about.

Try different ways of getting switched into the receptive mode, use a variety of scrying glasses. Help your companion learn by asking what they can see. Record or write down any images and information for later reference. Don't give up if results aren't seen immediately. Be patient because you are using a new skill and it is bound to take a while to master it. Suddenly, when you least expect it, the pictures will be there – and that is only the start of this useful ability.

3.
THE NATURE OF HEALING

Being well and in good health is a natural state, and it is only when something goes wrong that illnesses can afflict us. This simple statement may surprise some people who have never thought about the matter. It is only when our well-being falters and the thoughts of hospital, medicines, operations and so on loom on the horizon that we begin to worry about our health. To a magician good health is an important aspect of his or her character. As healing has many magical associations and many witches and other occultists offer advice or treatment it is very serious if they look like walking adverts for 'Your Life in Their Hands'! Your health is something to which you should pay serious attention because if you are going to offer help to other people they will judge your success by your own state of health.

Although Nature can drop trees on people, strike them with lightning or drown them at sea, most of the plagues, epidemics and serious illnesses which afflict mankind are assisted by our life-style, or our lack of hygiene or simple common sense. Today there is plenty of sound evidence that certain habits can prove fatal; that junk food and unnecessary anxieties leading to reliance on artificial medication can lessen a patient's life span, and certainly diminish the amount of enjoyment and pleasure he may get from life.

Today many people suffer from stress of one sort or another and lay at its door many of their problems. If you think back, our ancestors in the Stone Age must have been just as anxious, looking for shelter, attempting to hunt for food, or simply maintaining a spark of fire on their journeyings so that the clan would not freeze to death in the winter. Their worries were of a life or death variety, and the stresses of inter-tribal relationships such as concern about the safety of some new food item, uncertainties about the prospects of future shelter and the loss of a knowledgeable member of the clan must have been deeply sensed.

What has become very clear in the last decade or so is our search for alternatives to a number of conventional parts of our lives – in religion, in education, in spare-time activities and in healing. At this time when the unifying strength of the Age of Pisces is giving way to the more independent, individualistic current which will typify the Age of Aquarius, people are making choices for the first time in their lives. Before, they had often felt they were in the hand of 'authority' or 'the State', and had to accept this pattern for their birth, education, job, medical treatment and entertainment. Now this rigid structure is giving way, under pressures beyond its own making. Within the cracks new ways are beginning to put down roots and flourish, just as the weeds do in a derelict building. Many of these alternatives provide genuine chances for a new self-awareness, real and permanent healing and religious experiences previously undiscovered.

The first task of any magician is to come to terms with who and what he is. If you know you have bad habits, eat an unhealthy diet, keep going on gallons of tea, black coffee or by taking pills of some description, then you must consider this before launching yourself into a career as an 'all-knowing healer'. If you are coughing your lungs out over a cigarette whilst trying to advise some other person about his problems, or need to rely on chemicals to give you the strength to sit down and meditate, you will have to apply first the adage 'Physician, heal thyself'.

It is not necessary to reject any system of healing. Antibiotics can save lives, as can surgery, but many conditions which cause long-term suffering and unhappiness may be treated by some of the alternative therapies, which also include magical methods. One aspect of the Aquarian Plan is that we must find ways of living in closer harmony with the Earth beneath our feet, and with Nature, the Goddess or life-giving power which shapes

our mundane destinies. Nature can provide a wide variety
of cures, from herbs and 'simples' to teaching us how to
manipulate the life-forces in the Universe to bring healing,
peace and joy to those who suffer.

The Healing Power of Nature

How much of Nature gets into your life? Do you live in
the country, grow your own fruit and vegetables? Do you
walk through unpolluted fields, drink from sparkling clear
springs, breathe deeply air which is sea fresh and filled
with vitality? You lucky thing! Most people live in towns
and cities; struggle along congested streets where trees
attempt to survive the atmosphere and the council tree
surgeons; take exercise in indoor swimming pools of
chlorinated water, or jog through dusty parks. Most of
them survive to a ripe old age, and enjoy many aspects of
their urban existence too! Nature is not absent from
built-up areas, her healing powers are still available to the
town people, but they have to make a greater effort, and
seek quiet places where trees and plants grow unmutilated,
and where the light of the sun and moon may be seen
without the lattice-work of high buildings, man-made
structures and orange street lighting.

Nature is willing to share her healing power with us, if
we can take a few steps in her direction, learn her ways and
apply this knowledge, so well-known to our rural ancestors,
in ways which fit our technological life-styles. Everyone
can tell the difference between day and night; you can
generally decide if it is summer or winter, and if you look
at the night sky long enough you might be able to
recognize the phase of the moon and decide if she is
waxing or waning – that is the beginning of using the tides
of Nature to bring harmony and health to your own life.
Every aspect of the solar year, or the lunar phase, or the
tides of the sea has a force which can be used beneficially.
Just as it is possible to observe a seed put forth a shoot,
grow into a tall plant, flower, fruit, set seeds and then
decay, we can learn to discover this same pattern in our
own affairs and situations. Every enterprise tends to go
through a sequence of changes, be it the course of a
disease, settling into a new house, or finding and fitting
into a different occupation. In some cases the seed to fruit

cycle is very short, in other instances it can take years or even decades. When you start to apply magic to situations you should first discover which point in the cycle circumstances have reached, for each needs the application of the correct remedy. Sometimes it is necessary to build up strength, collect material objects or accrue information; at other phases it is important to throw off links, to irradicate factors or drive out disease. If you act in haste, or apply the wrong force at a critical moment in cosmic time you can waste your efforts or even make things worse.

The Sun

The power of the Sun is concerned with life – we wouldn't exist on Earth at all if it were not for the precise interaction of sun and earth, heat and radiation, gravity and distance which ensures the dynamic balance of our solar system to provide conditions suitable for evolution here. This is a delicate balance, and not immutable. The light of the sun provides us with a genuine healing ray, yet too much sunshine can be harmful to the skin. Sunlight helps us make vitamin D, necessary to health, and generally makes us feel brighter, happier and well. The Sun has been worshipped either as a God (and in some places as a Goddess), or as the symbol of a God visible to us on earth.

To use the Sun directly as a healing force requires little in the way of equipment or preparation. If you are unwell yourself, then merely sitting relaxed in a sheltered spot, and imagining the light from the sky shining through you in brilliant white-gold rays, driving out the darkness of disease, bringing relief from pain or stiffness, can be sufficient to get your own inner healing processes going. If you have a sick friend, tell them to do the same, allowing them to sit calmly in a sunny place as you explain how the vitalizing beams of light can help to set off the healing process, and drive out infection. This technique uses relaxation (which is very important in nearly all healing), and the imagination with which something symbolic of the illness can be overcome and driven out. Clinics treating cancer patients are now recommending a diet of natural fruits and raw vegetables, without salt or other additives; they teach relaxation exercises and the application of the will to get better, applied through the creative visualization of the cancer cells being eaten or destroyed by the patient's own auto-immune systems. This method of natural healing has had many successes when applied seriously to even very severe cancer conditions. As a rider to this, if you eat a large proportion of raw fruits and vegetables in your diet, add no salt or other chemicals (although herbs and spices are recommended for flavouring), and try not to be overweight, you will lessen your chances of being afflicted with cancer and many other complaints. Add a little exercise such as walking, dancing, swimming, riding, cycling or aerobic movements and devote at least one period of time every day to meditation, deep relaxation (not nodding off in front of the television!), creative visualization or any other similar activity, and you ought to be able to live a very healthy life!

The Moon

The Moon, too, has important applications in health. She is more directly concerned with your psychic life, she influences the pattern of dreams. In women, although their cycles may not exactly fit the moon's phases, she will to some extent affect their menstrual cycle, fertility and sexuality. Recent research by Dr Jonas of Czechoslovakia shows how the moon's phases combined with information on any woman's fertility cycle can provide a safe, effective and drug-free method of contraception; or for those who wish to conceive a child, can determine the best day to make love with this in mind, and even choose the sex of the baby!

Everyone can watch their dream pattern change with the moon phases, often peaking with vivid, colourful and interesting dreams occuring within a few days of the full moon. During the waxing moon it is a good idea to work magical acts which are growing, increasing and working in the outer world. The waxing moon can be used in healing rituals as a symbol that as her light grows brighter the life-spirit in the patient is increased and his body is better able to fight off infection or pain. With the waning moon the disease is felt to be waning too, decreasing in intensity and lessening its grip on the sick person. You can encourage the patient to watch the moon through a window, if possible, or in their imagination if they can't see the sky, and as the curved light of the moon changes, to feel its influence on their health. The moon is in some ways a more important symbol for her light can be seen both by day and by night, and the moon's shape may be seen in the dark sky, as well as during daylight whereas the sun only appears in a light sky! This may seem obvious, but light is a magical symbol of great significance, and the visible light of sun or moon or stars brings tangible forces which cannot be seen with the ordinary vision, but can be perceived in the imagination, or during meditations or rituals.

Healthy Living

You must become aware of the season of the Earth as well, because it is no help at all realizing you need a particular herb when the date on the calendar is December in the Northern hemisphere! Certainly herbs can be gathered at their most potent season and dried for later use, but many are far more effective whilst their life-force is still in them – the same applies to eating fresh produce. If it is still alive when you eat it you will be taking in the 'virtue' of that piece of food or herb, which will probably be beneficial to you. Cut out the chemicals you take in by carefully reading ingredients lists on packages. Even salt can change your blood chemistry, causing water retention which may put a strain on your kidneys. Of course, if you are living in a very hot climate and are sweating a lot, that is a different matter, but ordinary folk in a reasonable climate ought to bear these facts in mind when reaching for the salt cellar. Most people add salt to food without tasting it – so it is a habit rather than a taste preference which causes this action!

Much the same applies to sugar – we don't really need to eat the vast quantities we consume each year. Like salt, sugar is an additive to many ordinary foods; tinned peas, sauces and soft drinks often contain several spoonfuls of sugar in an ordinary portion, and if you want to balance your weight to your size, bear this in mind. Once you start reading the labels on tins and packets it is quite a revelation. If you do have a sweet tooth then using saccharin or other sugar-substitutes may not benefit your health in the long term. It is better to use the real thing in small quantities rather than take in chemicals which may again change your blood chemistry over a long period.

It might seem that all this information about food and diet, exercise and chemicals is a far cry from magic, but YOU are the key to the abilities you have. If you are addicted to sugar, salt or heroin you are not fully in control of your own destiny. To try to effect the patterns of the work of the world through magic when you aren't able to determine your own destiny becomes a pointless exercise. Most books deal only with magical arts, psychic skills and occult activities whilst ignoring the physical and emotional state of the magician who is trying to make these techniques work. Now we are becoming aware of the wholeness of all material reality, and maybe the invisible worlds of the inner, as well. If you change one tiny aspect of your life, in theory you are actually altering the entire universe! This is an awesome prospect for the novice magician to come to terms with, so it is important to begin making changes in something which is pretty well under your own control – YOU.

Healing Others

Once you have dealt with your own ills, allergies, addictions and anxieties through honest examination and, wherever possible, the elimination of the causes, you can attempt to offer healing to those around you. Perhaps if you have already found a magical companion you can start with them, or maybe they can practise healing skills on you. Anxieties may be dealt with by meditation. If something upsets you, examine it whilst sitting in quiet contemplation. You ought to be able to trust your partner not to discuss your feelings or doubts with the world in general, and you ought to be trustworthy too! Consider problems from all angles, take advice, and gradually a solution will emerge. This may not be an instant cure, but once it is found the results can be amazing and the whole of your life can take a turn for the better.

To work any kind of healing requires trust on the part

of the sick person and responsibility on the part of the healer. If you start meddling with the lives of other folk unasked you may find you are acquiring some of their karma. Even conventional doctors will not merely cure symptoms – for example, if someone turns up with a pain in the stomach the doctor won't just give them pain-killers and send them away, he will test them for infection and consider the possibility that the pain is a symptom of appendicitis, or some other serious internal condition. The magician must bear this in mind. By trying to alleviate the pain in a friend or relation, be it physical, emotional or psychological, it may cause them far more suffering, and the magician may also find himself burdened with their problems too. If a person asks for healing or help, then you should consider the matter very carefully before immediately plunging into a two-hour healing ritual. It is possible that the condition which needs attention is a lesson the individual has to learn, that some part of their nature needs looking at, and some aspect of their life requires sorting out. By all means help and, if possible, examine the situation to find a logical and lasting solution to these ills, but don't take on the burden of your friend relying on you, unless you are ready for it. Often a simple meditation can show you the crux of the matter, or maybe you can help your friend relax and see what underlies his current state, so he they can heal himself. In the long term nearly all healing comes from within, even if drugs, herbs, massage or surgery are needed to start off the healing process.

Suffering is not a requirement in learning, as it used to be thought. Religions don't need to teach its value in their creeds – we have enough to do coping with life's real situations without having the added penalty of suffering laid upon us. Certainly the child with the burned finger learns to be wary of fire, but the mother ground down with the responsibility of several children, ill health, lack of money and poor accommodation doesn't need to be told 'Suffering is good for you'! The most important lesson pain can teach anyone is that of avoidance. There is no reason to seek pain in order to gain spiritual insights – meditation in a comfortable chair can bring far more interesting revelations than being flogged with a knotted scourge. To open the doors to inner awareness a gentle approach is needed, not cruelty. A healthy and relaxed body and mind can provide far wider awareness of the inner side of life, and a greater understanding of the mundane world. Fasting, binding, pain and deprivation will not open the vistas of enlightenment in a controlled manner, though they might wring out a few tortured insights into the frailty of the flesh and the difficulty of obtaining eternal wisdom. Whatever methods you choose, do try to make them easy on yourself.

Methods of Healing

Once you have attempted to get yourself in tune with Nature, and so have begun to feel healthy you can decide what methods of healing you would like to apply. Certainly you can rely entirely on meditation to find the cause, and ritual to supply the cures, but the knowledge of some of the alternative methods of therapy by you and your partner will help in lots of cases. Several of the alternative techniques are based on magical rather than rational theories of healing, particularly radionics, homoeopathy and the Bach Flower Remedies which work so effectively on anxieties, fears and inner tensions. There are also a number of interesting methods which use massage, pressure or muscle testing which can be learned, in some cases from a book, or during a short course given by a trained expert. Do have a look at the introductory books on acupressure, which uses the points of 'meridians' which are lines of energy flow within the body, discovered long ago in China and Japan. In illness, some of these invisible channels are blocked thus cutting off the Ch'i or life-force from certain organs or systems. By massaging, applying heat, or after proper training, inserting fine sterile gold, silver or stainless steel needles in specific locations the flow of energy can be released and so a cure can take place. This technique works well for painful conditions, and acupuncture anaesthetics are used for even major surgery as they don't have the side effects some gas or anaesthetic drugs can have. Many of the massage points for treating headaches, anxiety, stomach upsets and other minor ills are on the hands or feet, and can soon be learned. Try these out on yourself and discover the effect

before working on other people, or allow your companion
to try to cure your migraine or bruised ankle.

Herbal Medicine
Herbal medicine has become popular again after many
years of neglect. There are plenty of simple herb teas
which can be drunk purely for pleasure and relaxation, or
to relieve tension, sleeplessness, 'women's troubles' or
fever. You will probable find new uses for the parsley,
sage and mint in the garden, apart from stuffing the
Sunday joint, for these can help a wide variety of minor
ills, and new herbs can easily be grown, even in sunny
window boxes, or on roofs or patios. Feverfew leaves
eaten in honey sandwiches can ease migraines, and this
daisy-flowered herb with its peppery scent is common,
growing wild in some places. Comfrey, dandelions, thyme
and camomile are useful, and any good book on herbs will
have clear pictures or photographs of these plants so that
you can learn to recognize them in the countryside. Many
garden centres now stock a wide range of these valuable
plants or you can buy packets of seeds. If you have any
spare seeds plant these on waste land, or in overrun
gardens so that they are available for others who might
need them. Again, share your knowledge with your
partner, make teas and bath mixes for each other to try.
Learn the applications of all the common plants, trees
and herbs in your area.

Homoeopathy
A more complicated application of natural substances,
(not only derived from plants, but minerals, tree bark and
even seeming poisons,) is homoeopathy. This is a fairly
new method of healing researched by Hahnemann in the
last century. He found that some substances applied in
minute doses sparked off a cure in sick people, but would
show their effect on healthy folk by giving them the
symptoms of the illness. Like appeared to affect and then
cure like. In ancient times there was thought to be a link
between a disease which produced spots and a spotted
plant used to cure it, and although homoeopathy isn't
quite this obvious, it can often genuinely cure long-
standing allergies, pains and complaints, even when other

treatments have not done so. To arrive at a medicine the homoeopath needs a great deal of strange-seeming information from the patient because the treatment is applied to him as a whole and individual person, rather that as a case of shingles, arthritis or gastric ulcers. It takes a lengthy training and very careful study to be able to apply the many hundreds of homoeopathic drugs, which are given in extremely diluted form to act as catalysts, which lead to a gradual and permanent cure. Often the illness seems to get worse when the drugs are first given, but this is a sure sign that the correct therapy has been found, for it recognizes that the body is fighting the disease, and that the symptoms prove this is occuring.

Bach Flower Remedies

Herbs and homoeopathy both work well when properly applied on physical illnesses, but the Bach Flower Remedies act on psychological ills. These very slow and gentle medicines are made from thirty-eight different flowers or trees and when taken over a period of time can assist in the recovery from fears, tensions and phobias which other treatments don't touch. Often these states can lead to muscular problems, allergies or depression which prevents the person being able to cope with life, or overcome ordinary problems. They can even be applied to things like home sickness, or 'psychic' attack if someone is afraid that another person has an unwanted influence over them. Many herbalists stock these remedies, or they can be obtained quite inexpensively, direct from the Dr Edward Bach Healing Centre, Mount Vernon, Sotwell, Wallingford, Oxon OX10 0PZ. Send a stamped addressed envelope for a list of the thirty-eight remedies and their specific applications. There are a number of books available too, explaining this effective form of therapy, which every magician should be aware of if he offers treatment.

Dowsing

Another skill every magician and his partner should acquire is that of dowsing with a pendulum. Get a small, symmetrical weight and a piece of thin twine or cord and teach yourself to allow it to react positively or negatively to questions you ask yourself. Hold this simple instrument lightly and ask a basic question, like 'Is it Wednesday?' You will soon find the bob swings slightly, either in a straight line, or a circle. Command your inner self, which is causing the muscles in your hand and wrist to move, to work harder. Soon you will get clear and decisive movements and can ask a question which has the opposite answer. Again your bob will swing in a different manner. Although some books imply there is a definite swing for 'Yes' and 'No' it does vary from individual to individual. Also, you may find if you ask questions about another person, or someone of the opposite sex, the swing answers reverse their code. Keep on practising with your companion until you can get firm, accurate and consistent results from this experiment, which although is being dealt with here in the healing section, has many other magical applications. Keep on trying until you are sure you can understand the code your own pendulum is using under different circumstances and then you can test it on healing situations.

You can experiment with lists of herbs, massage areas, Bach Remedies or forms of treatment with which you have become competent so that you can dowse along the list, picking out things to try in a particular case. You may need a sample from the sick person; a clipping of hair or nails, or a drop of saliva on a clean tissue will be sufficient to link you together whilst you investigate. If they are present you can ask questions whilst swinging the bob over their hands or you might feel more confident if they just supply the sample and allow you to work on their problem when you are feeling in the right mood.

Giving Advice
Quite often advice on diet, exercise, relaxation, new interests or dedication to getting fit can be sufficient to put someone on the paths to health, or the application of one of the massage techniques, like acupressure, foot massage, Touch for Health (sometimes called Applied Kinesiology), which relies on the tone of certain muscles to determine the state of the body and inner self as shown in the acupuncture meridians. You may suggest certain herbs to drink, to bathe in or to add to almond oil to make

a rub which can be applied to stiff areas, or for a general soothing massage which will be relaxing and calming.

Read widely, as there are plenty of excellent 'do it yourself' therapy manuals written within the last few years by successful practitioners. Experiment with a selection of different techniques, both physical and psychological, so that you and your companion have a repertoire to offer anyone who seeks help. In the section on rituals there are some which can be applied to magical healing, but often simple, sensible advice can put someone on the road to health. Anything which leads them to align their life with Nature, choosing natural foods, exercises and therapies, will not only assist them to get more out of life, but because they are a part of the whole cosmos, which is out of balance, their healing also heals the universe – that is why all magicians must bear their activities in mind and take full responsibility for their actions when healing or giving advice which may affect the life or future of any other person.

The Fountain of Light Exercise

One technique which is well worth experimenting with as an adjunct to healing is the 'Fountain of Light' exercise. In this, by imagining a set of colours up your body with the brightest, purest light above your head, from which you can draw a healing force, you can become filled with this health-giving power. Practise alone at first, or with your partner, until it feels natural and effective. Stand comfortably upright and close your eyes. Imagine that you are standing on a dark, black curved surface. It is so intensely black that you could almost imagine it is the night sky, spangled with brilliant stars. Moving up your body from your feet the colour changes to a dark, peaty brown, fading gradually as you move up your legs to a russet brown. At the top of your legs the colour is crimson red, in the sexual region. Above that is a band of orange across your stomach fading into a yellow band in the region of your solar plexus. Above the yellow the colour changes to a rich leaf green over the heart region. At the top of your chest and throat the colour changes through turquoise to a brilliant blue at the Adam's apple. From the bright blue the colour changes to deep indigo on the level of your third eye, in the centre of your forehead, and finally there is a change to brilliant violet at the top of your head. Allow these colours to become vivid and definite, and even if you are colour blind, or have difficulty in visualizing try to discover a gradation of tone, from very dark at the feet to a brilliant white light above the top of your head which you can imagine and use.

See the most vivid and shining whiteness as a great ball above your head and then imagine or perhaps even feel you can draw this force downwards through each colour band. As the light flows down through you sense it opening up a centre of healing and a balancing force, like a rose unfolding. The one at the crown of your head is the link with your 'Higher Self' through which you may work this sort of magic. At the forehead is a blossom of intense indigo which represents your psychic faculty. At the throat, as the brilliance flows downwards through your body, there flowers the blue rose of communication and speech. Below that there is a strange green flower at the heart centre, through which the power of love and compassion may flow out to others around you. Below that is the main healing centre of the solar plexus, through which the magical life force of the universe may be directed, in rays of sun-golden light, to those in need.

Below that, across your abdomen is an area of digestion and the orange-coloured flower which helps you cope with the mundane aspects of healing the sick, or will assist in digestive troubles. Below that is the crimson blossom filled with the brilliance of white light which enlivens your most basic urges of sex and true unity. This can be used to heal and balance your own life but it cannot pass out through its scarlet blossom a healing power to others until you have fully mastered the technique of opening and controlling this centre of energy. It is best not to try if you are a beginner as it can get you out of your depth if you are not truly balanced. Below that is a darker region of stability and strength. It is the strong stem on which the blossoms of sacred light grow, and it is rooted in the dark depths of the earth. This is the mysterious firmament which is why it may be envisioned as sprinkled with stars. When you are healing someone who may be sitting with you, first see the colours – black, dark brown, russet, crimson, orange, yellow, green, blue, indigo, violet – and then draw down the white brilliance. When you have managed to sense this down as far as the heart/green centre, pull it down to the solar plexus/yellow centre and open it as a great rose. Allow the same colour to flow through your arms and out through your hands. You do not need to touch the person at all but hold your hands close to them so that the fiery white/golden yellow light may flow over them. You will be guided intuitively how to go about this and will know instinctively when to stop.

At the end of the treatment imagine the white light changing to silvery rain, or a great sparkling waterfall which will flow over you, refreshing and cleansing you all over. Let this continue until you are certain all parts of your 'patient's' illness or symptoms have been washed away. Then imagine all the flowers closing one after another still retaining a spark of the brilliance within the heart of the closed flower. Start at your head, watching the petals firmly close over the glimmer of brilliance, which will bring you health and balance in between times, then close the rest in turn, in descending order. At the end you ought to feel good and not weary, for the energy of healing has been drawn from the great source of brilliant healing light and not from some resource of your own. Don't rush this experiment as it is very important, both to heal your own complaints and to assist other people. Get your partner to work on you so that you can experience the sensation of the healing force. It works on muscle pains, headaches, fevers and, if you are seriously ill and needing surgery, it can speed up the healing process of tissue or bones.

Psychic Activity

One factor of healing or at least advising which is more applicable to students of magic is within the field of 'psychic' activities. Many people, when they begin to experiment with esoteric techniques, find weird and upsetting things start to happen to them. Some go so far as to imagine that the moment they perform the first ritual some vigilant black magician is waiting and watching and will immediately lay a horrid curse upon them.

Certainly, when you awaken the sleeping faculties used in magical work for the first time some extremely strange things do appear to happen to you! You aren't under attack by some evil spirit, nor are you about to lose your eternal soul to the dark forces you have inadvertantly stirred up. You have opened those first doors to the inner world which has always been with you, but which you have been unable to sense before because of your own lack of sensitivity. Once you start to meditate, or perform the simplest spell, no matter how bad, feeble or inefficient your meditation seems to be, something on the inner will happen. You begin to sense the feelings of others around you, you become aware, without realizing it perhaps, of some of the effects which the interaction of individuals always make. Clearly, some of these links will be pleasant, others not so good, and these can make you feel vulnerable or under threat from some unseen presence. It is unseen, but it is really only part of yourself. No matter what occult fiction tells you, the 'Dweller on the Threshold' is just as much a part of you as your feet!

When you sense this guardian angel or advisor or inner self you may be overawed and so feel that something is 'out to get you'. Don't worry, you will get used to the feeling and not sense a threatening presence if you keep your head and meditate upon it. The inner self is a wise and helpful companion, so value its nearness, and learn the stillness when you can turn the threat into safety and protection. Black magicians are too busy trying to destroy the world and aren't likely to waste time or effort on attacking small fry like experimenting magical students, so get on with coming to terms with your inner self, and don't try running. After all, you will never escape your own shadow!

Certainly there are situations when you can come face to face with unpleasant 'vibes', or be in the presence of sick people whose aims are destructive and harmful. You may need to help sort out 'haunted' buildings or alleviate the sad, lonely atmosphere which can linger after an old person dies after a long illness, or at the scene of a horrific road accident. These acts are not for the novice, and it is wise to seek expert help before trying to shift a stubborn ghost, or nasty atmosphere. You may certainly try to improve the vibes of a new home though, or wipe the attachments from a second-hand item you wish to use, without too much previous experience.

People who fear they are under 'psychic attack' very seldom are, but if something has really scared them, it will take a lot of effort on your part to advise them to relax and allow their common sense to take over. What they feel may be very real, and their fears will build this up to a great unpleasant ghoul which seems about to get them. You will need to be very calm yourself, with your own psychic whiskers feeling for any actual nasties around. Definitely get your companion to help you calm down the 'victim' and try to discover what they have been up to. Many psychic upsets are the result of playing with inner matters, like using a ouija-board, or trying to get messages from the dead, or attempting to set up a seance without knowing how. Again these things will often open a crack between the ordinary self and the inner one, and if people have fears or phobias, or a lot of repressed and ignored memories of unpleasant events, these will be the first through the gap.

In the hands of trained and competent magicians some of these methods of contacting the inner are valid and quite safe but, like matches in the posession of small children, they can be extremely dangerous. Don't dabble, and try to prevent others from playing at psychic games because they always produce surprises, some of which are hard to ignore because they are not pleasant. Messages like 'You are going to die', true though they may be, are extremely upsetting to the average person, and can even lead them to make mistakes whilst driving, or may distract them when in a potentially dangerous situation, so that the ouija message becomes a self-fulfilling prophecy.

You may find a basic consecration ceremony will help. Blessed salt (for earth), water, a lighted candle and some incense are carried clockwise round the person, his room or house three times to banish fears, and actual presences. Imagine you are sweeping out bad vibes, old fears and lurking memories as you walk round with your companion. Then fling open the doors or windows so that daylight and the healing power of the sun can shine within. If the sun isn't shining that day, imagine it strongly flooding in with pure golden-white rays, lighting up dark corners and bringing a breath of fresh, pure air inside. Cats and dogs won't go into really evil places so watch the family pet. If it still won't enter the room refer to Dion Fortune's *Psychic Self-Defence* or the more recent book by Murry Hope *Practical Techniques of Psychic Self-Defence* which give detailed instructions on how to cope with any similar circumstances. Don't rush in to show off your new found psychic skills because you can get out of your depth. Do experiment by consecrating items or rooms for meditations or ritual work. Do learn to recognize problems and apply common sense, to healing or psychic matters.

Your Reactions
You will need to discover how you react to ordinary things like coffee, to common analgesics like aspirin and even foods or drinks. As your experiments in magic increase so should your awareness of these matters. You can get to the point that a single cup of instant coffee can keep you awake all night but on the other hand a large meal may not deaden your psychic sensitivities in the slightest. You can learn to control your awareness of your state of health. When feeling weary you can increase your energy through deep breathing exercises, or when feeling tense, by switching into an altered state of consciousness, in order to become relaxed in the dentist's chair, or before the important job interview.

If you suffer allergies to foods, or substances in chemical products or nature, dowse along a row of samples to locate the precise root of the sensitivity, and then see if you can locate an appropriate antidote or way of avoiding the effects these things can have on your life. You may find, when trying the pendulum over your evening meal, that some things you have always eaten are not good for you, lowering your energy level, or causing sleeplessness or irritation. This can be quite an interesting experiment because you may end up with a list of things to avoid, but equally you may discover foods or drinks which enhance your powers of concentration or energy. You might even locate a personal *'Elixir Vitae'* or a soothing substance far safer than sleeping pills or tranquillizers.

Observe Nature and see how she affects you. Watch

the weather and the phases of the moon and sun cycles to see when you feel alive, and when dull, when your dreams are bright, and your inner senses alert. If you are going to celebrate magical festivals to mark the passing seasons you will need to learn the dates and what is happening within you. Accrue information on new advances in alternative therapies and methods of healing. See how many 'old wives' tales' are proving to have grains of wisdom in them which, after being long ignored, are being rediscovered. Dig your garden and grow different plants and apply them to benefit your friends, brighten up your menus, or provide healing teas, baths and massage oils. Read the books on trees, and listen to the wisdom in the voices of birds, the wind in the grass, and the trickle of water. Study the weather and your inner feelings so that you can become whole, with all of Nature.

4.
CREATING A MAGICAL TEMPLE

If you seriously want to work magic and perform some of its most effective forms of working, you will need somewhere to do it. This place may take one of a wide variety of physical forms and obviously will depend on your purpose, resources and intentions. It might be a whole attic in a vast country house, a secret grove in a wild wood, the cellar of a city terrace, or the corner of your bed-sit. It may be a laboratory where modern arts of alchemy may produce from the unity of two opposites, within the heart and soul, the Elixir of Life. It might be a beautiful classic temple, carved in marble and decked with the Gods and Goddesses of the ancient world. Perhaps you seek a natural secluded grove, for the word 'temple' is probably derived from the trunks of holy trees whose stems have now been transmuted into corinthian columns of stone, or the groyned vaults of early chapels. You may work through meditation and vision so that your working place is an island of dreams in the tossing ocean of the mundane world. Your practical skills may become paramount so that you have a workshop and your altar is a bench or drawing board whereon you redesign the universe. It could be as small as a cupboard into which you retreat, hermit-like, to explore through the inner perceptions the entire cosmos, or a section of an ordinary dwelling wherein the angels venture, and spread their knowledge all about you.

No matter what its physical form or size, it will have several other counterparts, for the temple is 'not built with hands', it is built with love through the skill of the trained imagination. Once it has been set up, and consecrated in your own way, you may find some spirit will be indwelling there, ready to guide and instruct you. You cannot make this contact with the unseen by will power, nor by astral bribery, nor by any sort of threat or compulsion. If you make ready the place and send out a message through your inner self perhaps your Holy Guardian Angel will turn up to assist you. Maybe the Gods and Goddesses you invoke will be seen in your circle, or the powers of healing, knowledge and success will come to your special place and fill it with energy and life.

The Pillars of the Temple

You and your companion will be the pillars of the Aquarian Temple, no matter what other form it will take. Each of you represents in the world the dark and light posts which support the roof of your endeavour. In the past the pillars were inert, symbolic and static, but in the New Age they will need to move and flow and mingle their forces, expressed through human action within the arts of magic. There are plenty of books on the symbolism of the pillars of Solomon's Temple, of Hercules, and so on, but you are the support posts of the Temple of Aquarius, each bringing your own energy and ability. The men will have the strength in the outer world, the power of the Sun, fire and air, and all the things that such basic elements imply. The women will have the force on the inner levels where magic is real. They have the dark and changing Moon tides, the psychic skills and the attributes of the earth and the waters. Each of you will either be a God or Goddess, a power for good and an aspect of the total balance which is the harmony of modern magic. You will have to find ways, when working together of harmonizing and balancing aspects of each other's natures. You will need honesty, trust and consideration so that the two streams of power flow side by side. Imagine you are a pair of plough horses, working in double harness to plough a straight furrow, that your field may be well tended and the earth made fertile by your efforts.

To become balanced will take a lot of work because neither is the leader, for each of you will find a time to instruct and a time to learn. Each will develop skills which the other cannot match, and each will have successes and disappointments as the work proceeds. In the old alchemical texts the purpose of the very complicated process is to marry the opposites. These are usually thought to be silver and gold, or the great king and queen, or the lily and the rose. Each is a symbol of both a greater and lesser thing. In his explorations of alchemy, the great psycho-analyst Dr Carl Jung, began to discover parallels between states of consciousness and alchemical processes. He found that not only could you work at turning dull lead into shining alchemical gold, but you could turn the dim, confused consciousness of an ordinary person into the bright and shining awareness of the trained mind. He also felt that by uniting the outer male or female self with its inner and opposite female/male (anima/animus) a totally complete individual would be formed.

Many men are afraid of women and find it very hard, when set free from the chains of conventional religion, to be able to relate to a Goddess figure, or the female side of God, she who is Sophia (Wisdom), who can share her gift of knowledge and understanding with all who ask it. Once they can come to terms with this aspect of the power of creation many new doors will open up for them. The same may apply to women, who, after rejecting the pattern of 'God the Father' in all its possible forms, cling desperately to the Great Goddess to the exclusion of all else, including the fertilizing seed by which means she is a child of the mother. There is no simple way for any individual to understand the dual nature of the Creator, except to say that such understanding is very important to the work of the Aquarian Mage. Only by approaching the Goddess and the God through meditation or in the magical setting of a path working, by getting to know these forces both as outside influences upon your life and world, and also as components of your own inner being, can you fully grasp the work of the Mysteries.

Don't imagine that after a couple of attempts to visualize a certain aspect of a God or Goddess you will be completely ready to welcome them into your humble abode, or personality. That way lies the path of the ego, the dark road to disillusion and despair. You may be able to become a channel through which some aspect of the

Great Ones may work, but it is not for beginners, nor is it necessarily a pleasant or controllable experience. You will need to experiment with symbols, with basic exercises and traditional myths so that you can truly understand these powers behind the visible universe, and when you are ready, offer your dedication as their servant. You will certainly be accepted, but if you expect to be able to rule every aspect of your own destiny thereafter, you will probably be in for some surprises. Being the vehicle through which any great power manifests is not a game for novices, for as it says in many traditional lodge rituals 'My office is greater than I am and I strive to be worthy there-of'. The forces of the universe are a good deal greater than we are, and only by knowing who we are, as the adage 'Know Thyself' over the door to the School of the Mysteries in ancient times suggests, can any of us hope not only to serve but to survive the experience!

This is another reason why a respected and harmonious partner is so vital to the work of the Aquarian magician. In the last era of magic there were learned schools, well set up lodges and wealthy scholars who could spend their time studying ancient texts and trying out antique rituals. Today we are living in a new world and a new age. The old knowledge cannot help us in the computer age and the books we need to study may not have even been written, yet! The new magic is very different from the old, and rather than relying on lost languages and ancient symbols it uses the instrument of the trained human mind, which potentially, has access to far greater stores of information through the Collective Unconscious of Jung, called the Akashic Records in past ages. Either way there is far more information available to those who can learn to enter the state of mind in which it can be approached, and retain in memory whatever has been discovered there. That is the main task of the Aquarian magicians. Each must find ways to journey into this store of information and draw from it such understanding as each may safely carry, and then apply it in the world, so that through the alchemy of experience, mere information is changed into the pure gold of applied wisdom.

To continue this work you and your companion will need to set up a suitable Temple, Laboratory, Workshop or Grove, depending in which sphere you most wish to delve. Within that consecrated space, which may be enlarged on the inner to include the entire cosmos, or condensed to become within the whirling electrons of a single atom where the matter of creation dances eternally, you may discover the key to the universe. Which particular aspects of magic are most important to you and your companion will depend on your previous knowledge, and on your personal preferences because this is a large field of enterprise. You may fancy ritual or the arts of making talismans. You might wish to study healing or draw nearer the God and Goddesses of the pagan faith; you may prefer simple meditation and the gentle ways of pathworking; or study of lost knowledge and its application in technological times. Your individual purposes will to a certain extent influence the way your magical place is designed in the real world although, as you will have discovered through some of the earlier exercises, you can change its inner appearance and structure at will.

Furnishing Your Temple

Because this work is concerned with experiments in Aquarian magic the final place may be the result of experiments which you have not yet tried and so the pattern may need to remain flexible and open at present. This might even be how it stays. In any case, you will need enough space for you and your partner to be able to sit comfortably, and if possible, move around a central table, altar or work-bench. In the Golden Dawn days temples were furnished with Victorian gothic armchairs on daises for the principal officers, and the altar often had a chunk of marble on top. In the age of melamine and Formica you can still have your black basalt-looking altar, but you are also able to lift it! The things that are most important are the chairs in which you each sit, as many meditations, pathworking trips and certain experiments in time and astral travel will require you to remain still and passive for some considerable lengths of time, so comfort and convenience are important. Looking at what is readily available I have discovered that some of the high backed 'garden' chairs make ideal magical thrones. The angle of the back may be adjusted, and if you want the thing to fit in a particular colour scheme you can throw a cloth or blanket over it. These chairs are light to move about, and will fold up when not in use. By testing those available you will find one which suits your height and is supportive in the right places. Later on, if you wish to adopt a reclining position for some experiments it is easy to change the angle of the chair back, and foot rest.

You can use these chairs if you intend to work out of doors. They won't look out of place in the garden as that is where they were designed to be used. You may need to sit on a tree stump if your sacred grove is a long way from home but you may well discover that brief visits to an actual holy forest can be replicated in the laboratory by using the creative imagination, and you won't be bothered by gnats or the weather! Magical ceremonies held out of doors are extremely powerful but they tend to be the dynamic dancing celebrations of the ancient festivals rather than the static mental journeys of exploration which many prefer. Try it for yourself and see which gives you the greatest pleasure, power and results. After all you are an experimenting magician so you cannot settle for the first situation or test you attempt.

Symbols for the Temple

You will need some symbols, but again because of the new current of magical training, it isn't possible to simply say 'Embroider the Qabalistic Tree of Life in the Queen scale on a silk banner and hang it on the eastern wall of your temple, set up as in Dr Ignatius Golightly's book of 1809'. You will be testing new symbols and experimenting with forms, designs and images which are even now being formed in your consciousness. Certainly there are some symbols which appear to be important indications of balance but how you make these, and where and when you use them will be something for you to discover for yourself. Maybe you have other ideas.

As the table/altar in your new age temple is a workbench it would be best not to clutter it up with instruments, candles and statues except when these are needed for a particular working. If possible you could use the top of a bookcase, a shelf or low cupboard as the focus of your imagery, and maybe use the wall behind it to hang a poster, mirror or banner which is important to your present experiment. By using a length of cheap roller blind, or by making one with the discarded cardboard tubes (often found outside fabric shops), round which you attach a length of suitable material, you could create a scene, image or symbol for the work in hand. You could paint or embroider a representation of your God or Goddess, if you have the skill, or make a montage of images from magazines. You could have an enlarged photograph of some sacred place printed onto the blind, or make a design with cut-out cloth, stuck on with rubber solution so that it depicts the entry to a holy place, or a vista of an ancient temple. Use your imagination and your mutual skills as artists or creators of a suitable image on which you can focus. It could even be a picture of your real home so that it acts as a safety valve during workings and will bring you quickly back to the here and now. On your altar you should have a rock or slate or piece of wood which can be an earthing point too; just as electric circuits have their earth wire, so should magicians.

Sometimes you will need to sit side by side, facing this symbolic image, at other times perhaps you will prefer to be across the table, at right angles to it. Obviously the amount of space available will dictate this to some extent, as will the presence of other people, for two is the minimum, and seven probably the maximum for a group of novices. (If some of you are already senior initiates this rule won't apply!)

The other important matters to consider include the four elements of Earth, Water, Fire and Air, for it is the balance between these forces both as symbols, and within each individual that the strength to handle the vast powers of magic can be developed. There are usually several sets of items associated with the four elements: the rock, log, pentacle or shield which stands for Earth; the cup, chalice or grail which contains Water; the lantern, candle or bonfire which is the element Fire; and joss sticks, scented flowers or, best of all, proper grains of incense, burned in a thurible or chafing dish for Air. Previous authors have varied this arrangement and given different attributes, but this is a safe and effective set-up if you are a novice. Once you get used to the symbols you can change them if you want to. Many ceremonies involve a magical feast or Mass, and for these you will need consumable versions of the four elements, most often bread and wine, (or for non-alcohol drinkers, apple or grape juice). Salt is frequently sprinkled on the bread, or it is dipped into the salt before being eaten. In order that Fire or Air may be shared you have a choice of warming your hands over the candle or lamp, or sniffing the incense. In some workings a scented flower, a rose or lily, etc., is placed on the altar so that its perfume may be attributed to Air.

What you eventually choose to do will obviously depend on the state of your knowledge, the tradition in which you are working and thus the symbols which it employs. If you have the creative skills between you, and a place which may be totally dedicated to magical experiments you can decorate the room to represent the kind of Temple you really wish to work in. If you would prefer to work out of doors but circumstances prevent this, then by using tree branches, cut in the winter and decked with artificial leaves (the real ones dry and drop off!), you can form a tree canopy by stringing them from the ceiling. You will need to locate the load bearing joists first, though. You can carve trunks from pieces of waste polystyrene with a hot wire or sharp knife. You could also cut out mock trilithons and when painted with several coats of stone paint in various natural shades these can make a very realistic miniature 'Stonehenge'. You might find some shop display pillars in one of the classic forms to encircle your room (for the Aquarian Temple, like most of the oldest ones, is circular). If you have a green or brown carpet or even marble-type lino and can manage to paint the walls to represent a landscape at the bottom and a blue sky above (day or night as preferred), you can replicate any sort of sacred place you desire. Using white LEDs you can even have stars that light up! Visualize the ideal and then apply your creative skills to make it real. Books on theatre design will give you hints on what you can do with papier mâché, chicken wire and paint, discarded packing materials, plastics and superglue.

Costumes
Unless you are both totally happy to work naked in your

temple, some sort of costume will be useful. A simple T-shaped robe is easy to make from a strip of wide material cut to fit your shape loosely. You could simply fold a strip in half, cut a hole for your head, gather up the spare material on each shoulder with a double running thread or elastic, and tie it together round the waist with a cord, to make a serviceable tunic which suits both men and women. Of course you can be much more elaborate, but it is a matter of personal choice. You might like to have different coloured belts to match the colours of the planets, or some sort of head-dress, and a pair of sandals or slippers. Each garment has an esoteric meaning, which you will find in any prayer book which describes the items of ecclesiastical attire. Whatever you choose should not flutter over lit candles or bonfires and endanger you, and hats etc. should not blow off in a wind or tip on to the altar if you bow your head.

When you have collected all your bits and pieces do look after them; they aren't for wearing to fancy dress parties, and your Temple ought to be a special place, set apart for ritual work, not to be displayed to all and sundry. Once everything is consecrated it is 'set apart' for ever!

Setting up a Temple takes a long time so be prepared to take it slowly. If you start with something comfortable to sit on, and perhaps a poster, picture or symbol which appears to act as a doorway to you both, then you can call for help and guidance from your inner self, or from whatever Goddess, Deities or Powers you feel most helpful. Meditate and work through paths which lead you towards your ideal setting so that you build up information on the inner as well as collecting equipment on the outer. You might need tools and materials for talismans, or books, as well as a selection of coloured candles and safe candlesticks to burn these in. You might seek out a pleasant goblet to drink your wine from, and a food platter, carved of wood or hand-made pottery, or maybe you have the skills to make these yourself. The greater your involvement with every item used in magic, the stronger your links with it in its symbolic application and so your greater control.

Elemental Weapons
In the last generation of magical temples the four

elemental weapons played an important role in their consecration, rituals and symbolism but perhaps now is the time for a change in this respect too. Most magicians collected a Cup and a Sword, created or painted a Pentacle and dedicated a Wand, in accordance with the Key of Solomon or the instructions published in the texts derived from the Hermetic Order of the Golden Dawn. Each of these instruments has a large body of attached correspondences and you may wish to follow the well-trodden path of earlier magical practice. An alternative, which might align closer to the purposes of Aquarian magic is to certainly find a cup which you will need for the wine or water, and to make a personal pentacle, showing your magical aims and mirroring your current state of advancement. Swords have always been difficult to find, expensive to buy, complicated to make and rather embarassing to carry about if you are not performing rituals at home. Although it is possible to get a fake sword to hang on the wall or wave about during ceremonial consecrations etc., it might not feel right for everyone. Think about what you feel is most helpful for the sorts of ceremonies you intend to perform.

If you want something which might fulfil the task of the ritual sword yet is within your capabilities to make (one for each of you) design a long wand or staff. You will need a pole about 1 inch (2.5 cm) thick and about 6 feet (2 metres) long. If you are going to be indoors you will also need a support for it, made out of a large tin. Wrap several layers of card round the bottom of the pole to form a tube longer than the tin is deep and anchor this tube in the centre. Fill the tin with clean stones, sand or gravel and then top it with some runny crack-filling plaster. Leave this to set at least overnight. It should be heavy enough to hold the pole upright as long as no great weight is attached to the top of it.

This staff is your personal Staff of Life, and so it ought to be decorated with paint, ribbons, carving or appliquéd felt shapes to demonstrate your purpose. Should one of you be working alone, the Staff can stand in for your partner, or you can compose around it during a pathworking the image of your ideal God/Goddess. Perhaps from light card you can cut out symbols which can be slid over the top of the pole to represent various forces, for example a Sun and Moon, or the sigils of the planets. One staff could be basically silver and the other gold, or they could both reflect the colour between green and blue which seems to be associated with work concerned with the Aquarian Age. You should be able to take it out of its supporting pot (which should also be painted and decorated to fit in with your purpose).

You will probably need a cupboard to keep your material in, and an electric point so that you can run a cassette recorder for music during rituals or perhaps with the words of pathworking narratives prerecorded. It is often useful to record details of any ritual, and any messages or inspiration received during meditations as speaking requires less effort than writing, if you are very relaxed, or in an altered state of awareness during your workings. It is useful to be able to dim the lights, because although candles may be magically acceptable, if you have to read a script in their flickering light the only thing you may get from all your efforts is a headache. If you can learn to make use of all the space in your room so that the consecrated circle is actually larger that the physical space there is no reason why one of you can't lower lights, turn on tapes or music, or anything else still within the special place, by remote control.

Maybe your holy place is the Grail Castle, or one of the Temples of the Nile, or the Sanctuary of Poseidon at Sounion in all its sparkling glory, above the sun-bright sea. Perhaps you have recreated a grotto, with rocks and trees, or the Chapel in the Green, a circle of standing stones, or the entrance to the Underworld as created by the many builders of ancient earthworks, called tumuli, barrows or burial mounds. Maybe you have designed a star-studded astral Temple, or the control room of a rocket ship to explore inner space, or a quiet, womb-like sphere where the influences of the Great Mother can be encountered. Whatever symbolism and material you have chosen you will soon find that every ounce of effort was worthwhile, and that the time involved will quickly be repaid once you begin to make use of this 'other place' which you have created. Gradually you will find its atmosphere changes, and that simply to enter the place, adopt the robes, regalia, or even the frame of mind in which magic is a reality, will cause you to shift into that altered gear where your power and understanding may be awesome.

Treat all your equipment with respect, keep it clean and ready for use, ensure that the atmosphere of the Temple is not disturbed by entering it in a bad temper. Cool down first, and allow your magical personality to fill you. Look after your health, and by standing upright, with your shoulders back and down and relaxing the tension in your neck and back, you will find you feel a very different person – this simple exercise alone can be quite magical!

5.
THE PATTERNS OF RITUAL

One of the subjects which attracts some students to the arts of magic is the idea of ritual. The elaborate robes, the equipment and the theatrical performance of chanting words in strange languages and calling strange powers to do their bidding appeals to them a great deal. The truth of the matter is that, in today's terms, a magical ritual is more like the program in a computer. By entering certain information exactly, and in the correct order, using the language in which the machine is programmed, and interfacing with it properly, you will obtain the results you are expecting. Magic is the same. Instead of using Fortran or Basic, the magicians of past times would make their requests in Hebrew, in Latin or Enochian, the language of the Angels, (according to Dr John Dee in Elizabethan times.) Now it is much better to make all prayers, invocations and requests in your own familiar tongue. This will ensure that if an answer is received it will be in the same language, and you will be able to understand it!

A ritual is a way of combining the different state of awareness, (which you should master through the arts of meditation, pathworking and creative visualization first), with the equipment, symbols of the Elements, and the imagery of the 'other place' which you will have made with your Temple layout. In all systems, from those of the old, outdoor witches, to the most sophisticated lodge rooms of the Golden Dawn at the turn of the century, every group is aiming to enter a 'place that is between the worlds'. This is where the reality of the realm of magic can be approached most safely by those who live in the mundane state. Here you can confer with powers, discuss your life with your Holy Guardian Angel, receive information and healing, and accept the inner initiations which give your own abilities.

Each ritual will have a pattern and a purpose. The pattern is generally much the same, although it may be elaborated for more important workings, and simplified if you are alone, or just practising with your companion. The main sorts of rituals will fall into the following categories: active, where you are making something, consecrating a talisman, healing or celebrating a festival; or passive, where you are seeking information, perhaps through divination, pathworking or by direct inspiration. As you gain more skill and confidence, and as you and your partner make more of the equipment and see more clearly the path you wish to tread together, gradually your work will attract the attention of an inner link or contact with the unseen and this will add power to everything you do.

'The Dweller on the Threshold'

Because ritual can have a profound effect upon anyone who hasn't tried it before, it is a good reason not to rush into it the moment you have read the first book on the subject. As you adjust to the 'place between the worlds' you will become very aware of your own weaknesses and fears. This is often described in older books as 'The Dweller on the Threshold', and an encounter with it can be very frightening indeed. It is much the safest course to be well aware of any doubts, failings or actual fears derived from your previous experiences (in this current life, let alone earlier ones!) The Dweller or Shadow, to use Jung's term, is the hidden depths of your own nature, and contains the reverse, inwardly expressed aspects of your character. When you are seemingly kind and thoughtful towards others, your inner self may harbour feelings of cruelty or selfishness. You will have learned to come to terms with some of these darker feelings and so they will not bother you, but some may have been repressed, buried in the subconscious mind, and the first, basic acts of ritual fling open the door of their prison. This can give you a nasty shock if you are not prepared.

Another thing to bear in mind is that you will be dealing with forces which can shift the stars in their courses and direct the patterns of whole universes – not to be dabbled with by amateurs for an afternoon's entertainment! You will also, within the setting of even the simplest rite, be entering a paradoxical world where everything is true and nothing is proven. On the one hand you will be attempting to make changes, albeit small ones, in your own future, and on the other, aiming not to affect the lives of anyone else because that is unethical. It is a very narrow path, sometimes referred to as the 'sword bridge' in myth. Taking care with what you are doing before you begin can save you a lot of anguish at a later stage, and in magic ignorance is never a suitable defence!

The Group Soul

In the inner world of the magical Temple, whether it is a properly constructed lodge room set up by trained initiates to comply with a particular tradition derived from antiquity, or the eastern corner of your Balham bed-sit it can be a very strange experience, entering this special place and becoming one with its symbolism. You will also be sharing with your companion not only the work of constructing this Temple, but the offering of your own energies, and theirs, so that the combined work may be accomplished. In return you will both receive knowledge, strength and insights about your work from then onwards. This sharing with another person can feel rather strange too, because each of you has a natural flow of energy, a personal level of perception and commitment, and an individual perception of what is going on. Each of you will gradually have to learn the patterns of the other or others and blend in to one harmonious and comfortable pattern. Even two people can develop a Group Soul. It will eventually be through this shared yet deeper and wider level of consciousness that you will be able to enter, through regular ritual practice, the inner world of the reality of magic. You may seek knowledge from the Akashic Record, in which all human history is recorded, on such diverse subjects as for example the method and reasons for the construction of ancient stone circles, the ceremonies conducted in the Temples of Atlantis, and minor activities in your previous life before last as a horse trainer among the Mongol hoards! It is a source of great wisdom and any attempts to enter the Halls of Learning should be seen as serious journeys of exploration and inner awakening, not a casual stroll to fill in a rainy afternoon.

Of course, it is unlikely that your first assays in ritual work will have such profound consequences, especially if you tread carefully and step onto a well-worn path, but anyone who picks up some old book, and has a go, for fun, to raise spirits or call upon the dead can scare themselves silly because they do not realize what forces they are dealing with. People who play with magic for a joke, or pretend to be wiser or better trained than they are can end up in a very unpleasant state of mindlessness because without taking reasonable precautions they allow other entities to infest them, like mental lice, and these are not easy to shift. Certainly the average doctor in the mental health service is hardly likely to recognize a genuine possession or know how to deal with it. There may be many people who have played with this sort of fire who are now imprisoned by some aspect of another conscious-ness parasitically attached to what is left of their own mind. It won't happen if you are acting sensibly because the Gods protect those who seek proper knowledge and enlightenment.

Preparation for Ritual

The patterns of rituals can be changed to suit your immediate aims and needs, but generally there are the following points which ought to be considered:

1. What is the purpose of the ritual? You can't just DO ritual!
2. What is needed to make it work – people, robes, equipment, etc.?
3. When is the best time to do it? Consider ordinary matters as well as the astrological moment, days of the planets concerned and the correct time for the best results.
4. What sorts of results are you expecting? For example, a genuine physical healing, the arrival of a piece of

information or the specific answer to a prayer for a
new job etc.

5. How do you intend that the ritual be performed? Do
you know the symbols which are most relevant, or
the Goddess/God/Power whose help is required?
How will you contact them?

If your purpose is very simple and you have already
collected or made your robes and the symbolic elements
you will already be able to go into the planning phase.
Again, although an experienced ritualist can simply get on
with the action, beginners are seriously advised to plan,
understand and rehearse every aspect of a ceremony. This
will make the eventual performance ten times more
effective and a good deal safer than plunging in headlong.
A ritual is not merely the actual rite, but the build-up of
equipment, ideas and choice of symbols, God names and
objectives too. Every factor is important because, like the
computer program, each bit has a specific function which
is much greater that the thing itself. Time can be important
too. If you are celebrating a solstice, when the Sun stands
still at the junction of Sagittarius and Capricorn in winter,
and Gemini and Cancer in the Summer; or the equinoxes,
when day and night are equal between the signs of
Pisces/Aries in March, and Virgo/Libra in September,
you are aiming for a precise time when the sun changes
sign. This is shown in an ephemeris which is a list of tables
from which astrologers derive their data. You will find an
ephemeris very useful if you wish to discover days or
nights when certain favourable alignments of planets are
to occur. This is important in the case of initiation, which
is, after all, a mystical rebirth, so you may be acquiring a
magical 'rebirthday' complete with a new horoscope for
your magic personality, together with an occult name or
motto. It is also a good idea to consult the ephemeris if
you are beginning any project, for much the same
reasons. If you wish to perform a certain ceremony, a
quick look at the arrangements of the planets at the time
can give some hints as to your likely success, and perhaps
the manner in which this might be accomplished.

Pagan Feasts
You should be able to recognize the phase of the moon

from a glance at the night sky, and also know the proper dates for the old pagan feasts if you intend incorporating these into your system of ritual or worship. In pre-literate times festivals were set by what was happening in nature and not by some pre-ordained calendar date, as they might be now. Church festivals, except Easter which is still fixed by the moon (which is why it moves about so much), have been allocated to fixed dates, celebrating the life of Jesus or of the saints and so on. Many of these festivals are much older, beginning in pagan times as high points of the story of the Goddess of the Earth and her Lord, God of the Sky. Of course this pattern, reflected in the growth of crops and the activities of animals differs from place to place and country to country. If you don't grow corn you can't celebrate the death of the Corn King, and where vines aren't grown you can't have a vintage feast. You must look at your homeland and actually witness when the first blossoms of the hawthorn (May) are to be seen so that you can celebrate May Day!

The oldest feasts are linked with the Goddess and the God as parts of a story in which their lives reflect those of Nature, but because of climate, location and local soil these vary quite a bit from what the books say. Going quickly through the year, you begin with Celtic New Year which is about the beginning of November, or the solar year at the first point of Aries, or the calendar year, 1st January! You will need to decide which makes most sense to you and your friends. Anyway, the festivals which SHOULD BE BASED ON WHAT NATURE IS DOING NO MATTER WHAT THE CALENDAR SAYS, give you the following: Candlemas or the Feast of St Brigit, when the Goddess is welcomed back after the birth of her Son/Sun at Yuletide. It is the time for looking for a few of the first wild flowers in southern Britain, usually snowdrops whose white and green petals show they are linked with the White Goddess. Next, after the Spring Equinox, is May Eve or Beltane, a fire festival when cattle were brought from their winter quarters and turned out on the high mountain pastures. It is celebrated when hawthorn blossoms, again white, are to be seen. After midsummer and the longest day, you have the start of the harvest, Lammas (Loaf-mass from the Saxon, when the first new grain was baked into bread). Here the God as spirit of the Corn becomes Lord of the Under/Otherworld, a place of magic and eternal youth, and corn dollies are made to keep his spirit of fertility until the spring sowing. When the harvest is in and the Autumn Equinox and the Feast of St Michael (a very pagan saint) has gone by comes the fire feast of Hallowe'en, Samhain, the end of summer when all flocks and herds and family are gathered in for the cold dark. Games with apples, the fruits of the Celtic Tree of Immortality, are played. People duck for them in buckets of water, eat them from strings, or cast the carefully pared skin over their shoulders to form an omen of the first letter of a special person's name. Hazel-nuts from the tree of wisdom are eaten, and some are used to foretell events when cast into the fire, hissing or bursting as nature demands. If you think about it, dressing up, 'Trick or Treat' and many other games, including Bonfire Night with its fireworks can be traced right back to much older feasts and gatherings.

If you celebrate these, together with Yule-tide and Twelfth Night (when the Mabon, the young Sun King sets out on his journey, as champion of the Goddess), and either new or full moon, you will have plenty of occasions for rituals incorporating part of the legend, or the symbols of each, as well as its aspects of magic. Each ancient festival has certain magical activities or powers associated with it, and if you devote a little time getting to know the cycles of Nature, she will teach you her secrets.

Planning the Ritual

Whether your ritual is to be a religious celebration of a season, or just a working for a particular purpose you will find that developing it around a pattern will help you and your partner to achieve the steady build-up of force, and a greater awareness of your entry into that 'other world' of magical reality. You will find appropriate things to say or do (in fact you can mime an entire ritual to music, or dance it, or act out what you wish without saying a word, so you won't disturb the family or neighbours). The best for YOU will be those you have created for yourselves, rather than picking out someone else's invocations, taken out of the context they were part of, and mixing systems of symbols. This is particularly dangerous as some systems are not compatible, just as a computer programmed in Basic will not respond to commands in Algol or Fortran, and the incorrect instruction can wipe a program or blow up a chip! By all means, on different occasions, work with Egyptian God forms, or Qabalistic angels, or Celtic heroes, but don't try them all together – it's an explosive mixture. If you are a novice work in your own language, inventing or allowing yourself to be gently inspired by the Goddess of Wisdom in the art of ritual invocations and actions. Ask and you will be taught!

Here is a list of points to go through for most rituals. You will find them in older systems, but you can design totally new workings on a similar ground plan. First you must mutually decide your purpose and collect all the items you require, both as personal attire and symbols of the Elements, bread/wine/salt for the ritual meal (or whatever set or similar items you prefer to use), then follow these steps:

1. Bless yourself – something like the invocation on page 20 will do.
2. Bless the room, making it a holy place, by first asking that the symbols of Earth, Water, Fire and Air may purify and clear the atmosphere, and then carrying these symbols around, sharing the words/work with your companion.
3. Allow your magical personality to flow over you, perhaps during a short meditation, pathworking or similar exercise.
4. State the purpose of the working, and call upon the Goddess of the season, or the angel of the work or the power of healing, etc. This ensures that you and your companion(s) all know what you are doing, and can agree and focus on this aim.
5. Now is this time to actually tell the story of the festival, set out and consecrate the talisman, concentrate on directing a healing power, or allow yourselves to sink deeper into the inner atmosphere of your Temple so that you can receive instruction, guidance or inspiration. This may be helped with music, or by another pathworking, or by each

person in turn adding to the narrative. You may seek a Guide or the Goddess now.

6. Next comes the ceremonial sharing of the Bread and Salt and Wine. The Bread is the fruit of the Earth and the Salt represents the Mysteries which are hidden in all things, yet the magician can sense them and work with them. The Wine is both Water and Spirit for it is the culmination of the essence of the God. You may bless each item in the name of which ever Goddess/God/Angel seems most appropriate. Always offer the Cup with both hands, and accept it in the same way. Take a piece of bread or biscuit and dip it into the salt. Acknowledge in words or gestures that in sharing the sacred feast you are one with all nature. You may pour a few drops of wine and scatter some crumbs on the earth, or onto a dish of earth placed there for libations, as a thanks offering. Again wait to see if you can feel the presence of any holy forces at this time.

7. It is traditional to face each point of the compass and offer a prayer for such things as Peace in the World; for healing of those known and unknown; for harmony with the Earth and the force of Nature, and for a greater understanding of the Mysteries. Add any other ideas you may have, slowly and with sincerity.

8. Unwind the circle and allow the ring of protection to ebb away gradually. Feel a sensation of peace, awareness and harmony between you and with the whole world. Pinch out any candles, although a central flame may be left lit, so long as it is safe.

9. Disrobe and gently awaken to a new and clearer awareness, relaxed and fully conscious of anything which may have occurred during the ceremony. You may even KNOW by now what the result of your talisman, healing or other work will be, and when its results will be obvious.

10. Clear up and put things away. Cast out the libation bowl onto real earth, unless you have been working outdoors, where this pattern may be followed, but with less paraphernalia. In a glade you can use a

stone or tree stump for an altar, wands from trees as your ritual staffs, a rock for Earth, a little Water, a small, safe lantern for Fire and a smouldering incense pot for Air. Even in your Temple a sea-smoothed stone or river-rolled rock will be a useful item on which any power may safely be earthed. If it is too big to go on the altar, place it on the floor on the north side, where you can touch it with your foot or hand if necessary. (This can help you come back to reality after a simple meditation.) Climb a mountain and bring back a sacred rock or slab and with it the memories of its home.

Writing down rituals and sharing these can lessen their power, and you will discover that any prayers or ceremonial invocations taken from books will not feel as effective as those you have created for yourself. The same applies to equipment. You can order everything from an occult supplier but none of it will be as effective as the things you make yourself. Even if you are not very skilled at any handicrafts there is nothing to stop you learning by practical experience, and it is surprising what you manage if you try. One set of objects you and your partner might like to have a go at making are the containers for the elements. A pack of quick-drying modelling clay will make a set to hold incense sticks or cones, a candle, water and a flat dish or platter which is the symbol of earth. With a little ingenuity you can wind a small strip of clay around a pencil or wooden spoon handle and by carving the top of it with a pin, make the centre of a flower which holds the incense. Next, make a flatter dish with a thick bottom into which you can press a short, fat candle. The lower level will be a wider dish with petal edges and enough of a dip in the centre to take the water. The last piece of clay is made into a circle, about ½ inch (1 cm) thick onto which you can mark or later paint leaves and symbols. Each item should fit into the one below so that the whole form a flower, either the English rose, long associated with the Mysteries of the Rosy Cross, or the Eastern Lotus, with pointed petals and the flat, almost round leaves of water lilies.

6.
MAGICAL EXPERIMENTS
WITH TIME

'Eye-witness account of the Battle of Hastings' 'Temple of the Sun finally completed – architect explains 200 year delay . . .' 'Housewife remembers being Rameses II'. These are often the sorts of headlines found in recent books about past life recall, or in scoffing accounts in the newspapers, and they can detract from an important aspect of magical work.

Magic has always been associated with Time – recent research is confirming that the most ancient sacred sites have markers which indicate special rising or setting points of the Sun, Moon or some of the stars; especially many of the great outdoor sanctuaries in the British Isles and Europe. Time was magic, especially when the priests were able to predict the coming of eclipses, storms and important times in the farming calendar and so help their people achieve successful harvests and fruitful cattle. Magic is also associated with time in that astrology is one of the oldest arts within the scope of seekers of knowledge, and depends on the exact positions of the Sun, Moon and planets in relation to the Earth at the time of birth of a child, from which trends in his life may be worked out. Magicians have often used astrological data to discover the most potent moment when the beneficial planets are in line to perform some complex magical operation or ritual. They also look at the horoscope of a person who may have come for help to see if his 'bad luck' or illness could be in any way affected by the planets.

Most traditional schools of magic hark back to ancient times. They are based on the wisdom of Ancient Egypt, Chaldea, China, India or even Atlantis or earlier cultures.

People from the remote past were always considered to be more knowledgeable, philosophical or informed and this 'lost knowledge' is sought by many students of occultism. Witches try to prove their coven has its roots in the Stone Age, or that all legends of the Gods go back to a 'common hero tale' of some lost Titan or mythological king who ruled in Lemuria. Some students forget that knowledge is expanding all the time. We now know far more about the world, its people, customs and ancient skills than our grandparents could ever have known, and certainly generations before that had access to even less information!

However, the past does have a great attraction for seekers, especially now when the rational, standardized ideas of Pisces are giving way to the wider, free-thinking ways of the Aquarian Age. In the quest for personal identity, which is one of the first and hardest lessons of the true occult student, any application of successful techniques which leads to deeper personal understanding is worthwhile. It is for this reason that many people are now attempting experiments in 'past-life recall' by a variety of methods.

Past-life Recall

Some venturers into times past make this mental journey because they have fears and phobias and no amount of probing into events in this current life has been able to cast any light upon the origins of these anxiety states. Some people are convinced they were kings or pharaohs, priestesses or queens in previous lives and wish to find further evidence of their historical fame. There is a well-worn joke about the guests at a 'Come as you were' party all turning up as Cleopatra, Napoleon, Julius Caesar or Mary Queen of Scots. Sadly, many very ordinary people, in their current lives, do have these notions about their power and position in the past, but seldom do they exhibit now, the wisdom or strength of character their previous 'self' would have needed to stay in power.

Magicians often make this voyage into the unknown past because they are certain many of the occult skills they seem to show now, like clairvoyance, the knowledge of symbolism or the ability to handle the power of magic comes from advanced training in some temple school in the remote past. Many accept the fact that much of the lost wisdom of the past may be recovered if those who were living when it was first taught could remember what was shown to them. This applies in the fields of healing, especially as there is increasing interest in alternative forms of therapy, many of which (like acupuncture, for example) are extremely ancient. It is clear that a great deal of herb lore has been forgotten and that other techniques of massage, manipulation or simple plant medicine have been lost because they were not written down.

Some people are merely curious about who they might have been in the past, or if they in fact had any kind of previous existence at all. They are encouraged in their interest by the considerable number of published accounts, books and assorted media information on the exploits of other explorers of the inner world. Joan Grant set the scene a good few years ago with her 'novels' which she wrote as autobiographical accounts of her previous existences among the Temples of Egypt and the forests of the Red Indians, and so on. Others have followed a similar path, sometimes interweaving their memories with those of close friends, doctors or family, to build a complex web of relationships left over from hundreds of years before. The evidence is certainly mounting, but it would be unwise to accept every part of it without allowing your critical faculties to come into play. It is too simple to say that everyone who relaxes after a Sunday lunch and suddenly discovers he is in High Street, Jerusalem one spring morning is actually about to witness the crucifixion of Jesus the Nazarene; or that the ladies who imagine themselves the reborn Nell Gwyn or Lady Hamilton do so because of recurring dreams or images awoken by a good novel or film.

The reason for seeking information about past events in your own life track can probably be identified as one of the following:

1. Plain curiosity.
2. A genuine desire to uncover historical facts (which may not imply personal memory or reincarnation).

3. A wish to discover all that can be known about yourself as an eternal individual, including faults, fears and failings.
4. To see if you can uncover information or 'lost knowledge' in any field of past expertise, especially healing, science and magic.

It doesn't really matter under which heading your own aims may lie as the techniques readily available could be useful in any case, but if you don't feel personally involved in past ages, then you will be able to view any scenes or other information which you may encounter without necessarily being 'part of' it. Certainly people's experiences vary quite a lot, depending on what method is used to invoke the past to the awareness, and it may take a number of attempts before even the slightest indication that you are able to travel back in time is apparent. Also, it is worth while trying out different approaches even if the first one seems to get results.

Reincarnation

If you are going to start delving about into your previous incarnations, or assist your magical partner or a friend in this work there are a number of things you should bear firmly in mind before you begin. DELVING INTO THE PAST CAN BE VERY FRIGHTENING. Reincarnation implies previous DEATH and this is still a subject which scares people silly! Death in the past was far from pleasant – dying of disease, injury or battle wounds without the aid of modern painkillers and drugs – and if it is your last death you are re-experiencing then you may perceive a lot more sensation than you care to feel. When you actually enter a previous life you reawaken all your old senses too, so be prepared. (You can practise by remembering any frightening events in this life, like car crashes, accidents or serious illnesses, to find out how well you can remember and tolerate that memory before you tackle any greater adventure.) The same applies if you are helping someone else, because they can become very scared indeed if they enter a phase from the past when they were in danger, or dying and so on.

There are a number of other basic bits of information

to consider fully before you set out to open old doors of memory. The first is the time factor – I mean present time. You cannot fit in a quick session before a TV programme starts, before dinner, or after putting the children to bed etc. Time travel and exploration is a long-term and slow business. To reach even a state of mind where it is possible to go through time at all may take at least an hour, and once you do encounter a method which works you can spend hours trying to find out who you are and when you are living. And that is only the beginning! Logically, you must realize that to live through many of the episodes of a previous existence can take almost as long as the life in question. In practice, it doesn't take THAT long, but to analyse any significant amount of relived experience can take much longer than you might think. It isn't as if you can simply switch between then and now sequentially, either. The bits you recall will be fragmentary, scattered and incohesive, just as your memories of childhood are. Some events stick out clearly in your mind, even after many years, others are totally forgotten. For example, when did you first ride a bicycle or swim one length of the pool? What did it feel like to learn to write and what books did you actually read unassisted? Who was your first friend and under what ruler was your country then? In the past all these details could help you to pinpoint the era and place, the position and authenticity of your last life. It is the minor details of costume and climate, food and scenery which tell you that you are in eighteenth century London, or fifth century Italy, or tenth century China – you don't often find a newspaper to hand!

There are a variety of methods which you can use to try to awaken past life information, or simply rediscover historical events (from an 'eyewitness' viewpoint, if you don't accept reincarnation, genetic memory or any other continuation of the individual, immortal human spirit). Some of these are straightforward and can be begun alone, others rely very definitely on the assistance of one or two really trustworthy companions, who must be prepared to take notes or make recordings patiently and conscientiously for however long it takes to get useful material. They must remain calm and comforting if the time traveller is going through a difficult event, and help him or her to get back into present time safely and fully at the end of each session. This is no light undertaking, and ought not to be tried unless you are sure you can commit the necessary time and effort – either as the past adventurer or companion. Even if you begin your travels using one of the most basic methods, later on you may well require assistance to document and research any material you have uncovered, or to try different ways of dipping into the past which require the guidance of a companion.

Another thing to consider before you begin is whether you already have an inkling of when you were last on earth. Quite often images from childhood, or repeated dream-scapes can give you a clue. You may also have had experiences of *déjà vu*, that is a distinct feeling of having 'seen before' some place that you are certain you haven't actually visited. Often you can remember having a dream of the place before you arrive, sometimes a long while before, or you can describe what is round corners or inside buildings before you get there. It is possible that room settings in museums or antique furniture or old objects can spark off a memory as well. In fact, these can be used to encourage or confirm material as one of the experimental techniques which are recommended for you to try.

As well as a reliable companion or two (with whom you can exchange roles, allowing them also to explore the past if they so wish), you will need a good tape or cassette recorder and notebook. Although tape recorders are useful and generally reliable, sometimes the time traveller is talking too quietly for the microphone to pick up the words clearly. This may often be the case with machines with a built-in, rather than separate microphone. Also it is possible that some sessions may run on for longer than it takes to record on one side of a cassette tape. A brief note of information, a name, place, time, or detail of costume or food written down may be the vital key not transferred to the tape recorder. It is also much quicker to flick through written notes than to search back and forth along an hour or so of taped information. In some cases, the traveller's face, expression, voice and accent will change considerably and if you wish to record this evidence you might want to resort to a video recorder if one is available. Occasionally the time adventurer might want to draw or write so spare paper and pens should always be to hand. As the relaxed state which is best for receiving information can leave the experimenter feeling cold or hungry, a hot drink and a snack should be available so that he doesn't forget what he has discovered whilst boiling the kettle or rummaging for the biscuit tin!

There are a number of other things which, depending on your previous experience and skill in magical techniques, should be considered. it is generally thought that a witch's magical circle or the magician's temple is a place 'outside time', or where time is stopped or changed. Certainly, if you have been meditating successfully, or even merely day-dreaming, you will have discovered how time can slip by unnoticed. Sleeping too, switches off your sense of time actually passed, and dreams can appear to have lasted for several days, or during a sleepless night, the hours of darkness may appear to stretch for ages! This applies to your journeys out of time. If you are travelling you may be totally unaware of how long you have been away from present time, and it will be your companion who grows weary and gently calls you back at the conclusion of a lengthy session.

Techniques for Recalling Past Lives
In order to escape into the past in a way in which you are totally in control you will need to practise the different techniques to find which suits you best. The main ones are meditation and dreaming, when you are probably working alone and doing your best to record material as you remember it. Although these are suitable approaches for people with little spare time they do have snags. When meditating you cannot easily direct the line of your meditation without interfering with the flow of consciousness, and perhaps influencing the material which you later remember. In dreams you have even less ability to direct or control what you are apparently experiencing, and as mentioned before, some of the past life material can be very frightening. It is no consolation to your sleeping partner if you wake up from one of your experiments at four in the morning convinced you have

been shot with arrows, poisoned, or are dying of plague!

Methods in which the traveller retains control over his state of consciousness include magical hypnosis, the Christos technique, guided meditation or pathworking. Other methods can include psychometry, where old objects (for example, the standing stones in an ancient sacred circle, or tapestries from a medieval castle walls), may be felt whilst in a calm and relaxed state, and so pictures may arise. These don't necessarily turn out to be actual personal past life material, but it is an approach worth experimenting with. Again, by visiting those museums or stately homes where room settings give a clear feeling of past ages, and allowing yourself to sink into a quiet, meditative mood, you may discover clues as to whether that period seems familiar or not. Of course, your earlier lives may have been lived in different countries, cultures and levels of society, so visiting local collections or old houses may not help. None the less, it is worth exploring a variety of ancient places or getting the feel of old tools, jewellery or fabrics in case they do spark off that first bit of far memory from which a complete picture may eventually be built up.

Hypnotism

Although most textbooks on hypnotism suggest that the hypnotist is in control, in actual practice, within the magical (as opposed to the clinical/medical or psychiatric) application of the technique, the subject can determine the depth to which he will sink, and at what point he wishes to awaken. Although during the experiment he is willing to accept the suggestions of the hypnotist, whom he must like and trust and have already decided to co-operate with, he can terminate the altered state at will. Another misconception about hypnotism is that the subject is totally unconscious, that is 'asleep', when in fact, he may well be even more alert and aware than he is when not in that particular altered state. That is where the crux lies – it is an altered state of CONSCIOUSNESS! Obviously, it is not a technique to be applied without training and plenty of experience because it can be alarming to both the subject and the hypnotist if some unthinking suggestion is given which cannot be counter-manded, and the very relaxed subject may not feel able to return to a normal waking state unaided. Any serious book on the subject will give clear warnings as to this point. Also, any suggestions which imply the subject is losing control of his senses, his feelings or his body should never be given as they can cause fear and resentment, and prevent any real results being achieved. In the hands of a skilled and sympathetic hypnotist this can be one of the most useful techniques which assist the time traveller to make his first journeys of exploration. It also has the advantage that if he is given a key word or phase, he will be able to return to the state for further explorations without needing to undergo a lengthy induction process. Unless you are very sure that you know what you are doing, though, you should not use hypnosis nor subject yourself to the suggestions of an untrained individual.

The Christos Technique

The Christos technique was first described by Glaskin, in his book *Windows of the Mind*. Here there are three operators: one is the traveller; another massages the area of the third eye on the traveller's forehead, and the other person massages his or her ankles. It is then suggested that the traveller, who usually lies flat on a couch or the floor, is able to expand and then contract his or her length. After various other instructions are given, the traveller is asked to project his or her awareness out of the body to examine the outside of the front door, and then the roof of the house. Other suggestions of flying are given, over a fairly long period of time, obviously depending on the response to the previous instructions. Gradually the traveller is encouraged to fly away and eventually land at some distant place, both in space and time, and describe to the operators what he or she is able to see or sense. There have been many hundreds of successful trips of this sort made by meditators and students of magic in groups all over the world and a large percentage of them seemed to be able to transcend time and distance and explore other ages and places.

Pathworking

Another method, which for novices is probably the safest, is the use of pathworking. It has the advantage that it may be done with a group of experimenters who all want to see if they are able to travel outside time, to give them the chance to make an exploratory journey under controlled conditions. For this, many of the original criteria apply; that is plenty of time, a relaxed atmosphere, recording equipment including pens and paper, and a reliable and calm individual who is prepared to lead the group on their mental journey, and help any who stray off the path, or become alarmed at their experiences. Although an initial journey may be shared by a small group (not exceeding four travellers), later sessions using this technique ought to be on an individual basis. As with all pathworkings, plenty of time should be allowed for the experimenters to explore and experience whatever they come across during their mental archaeological digs.

Once all distracting noises such as the telephone and other occupants of the house have been silenced it is as well to have a few moments of quiet reflection and calming and relaxing exercises. Everyone tries to become mentally still yet alert and ready for the adventure to begin. Each should be seated comfortably, with his head and neck well supported so that he can breathe easily, and his feet should rest on the floor or some supporting books so that he is balanced. A little quiet music may be played to set the mood, and then the leader begins her narrative, which might go something like the following:

> You are all coming with me on a journey back through time. You will always be able to talk and to breathe easily. Whatever you see or experience will not harm you, and you may return here at any moment. Firstly I want you to fix your attention on the door to this room. Look at it now and remember it, and then close your eyes and allow yourself to sink down in relaxation. The reason to recall the door is that it is your 'way back'. If you become frightened, feel as if you are in danger, or you have had enough, simply see that door, as you did a moment ago, and then you will find yourself safely back here, alert and calm.

Speak very slowly, pausing between sentences both during the

*instructions and later on during the journey, so that everyone has
plenty of time to try to see or experience (some people feel, sense or
glimpse the scenes you may describe). Keep your eyes on the
experimenters so that you notice any signs of distress. If anyone does
look as if they are having a tough time, gently call their name and
remind them of the door to return by. Don't panic or shake anyone
who is relaxed or meditating etc., just continue to speak firmly and
quietly until they open their eyes and look alert – then continue the
narrative in this sort of manner:*

You are now going on a journey back through time to try and
locate an age or place where you lived in a previous life. If I
speak to you by name, please answer, as you will be able to
do, otherwise just observe or sense whatever you can. If you
get scared, look at the door and return here in your own
time. You are quite safe and this is an experiment which
many have safely tried before.

We are now travelling along a road which you know well.
As you go along you discover it is beginning to change from
the tarmac and modern buildings which you are familiar
with. There are trees and hedges and the pavement is giving
way to a rough earth surface, rutted and marked by horses'
hooves and the waggons they pull. As you walk slowly down
this road to the past, time is flying by you, and lost ages are
coming into focus. Gradually you will be able to see scenes
which were familiar to you in your last life.

*Elaborate this text as much as you wish, but try not to give direct
suggestions, like 'There is a lady in seventeenth century dress
coming towards you', or 'Some Vikings are carrying their battle
axes and shields up from their longship moored in the river'. Set a
scene which might suit any past age, or even place so that everyone
can create or remember details as he sinks deeper into this time
journey. Watch each individual and then ask them in turn, by name,
'John, what can you see?', 'Mary, is there a house nearby?', 'Bill,
are there any people where you are and what are they doing?', and so
on, round the group. Allow then time to speak as they may feel very
remote and relaxed. Record what each says. Some will experience
nothing, merely a feeling of peace and relaxation. Others may see
clearly and distinctly and be able to describe intricate details of
costume, scenery, activities and buildings.*

I want you now to look at any person you can see. Is it a lady
or a man? Are they working at something or standing about?

Are there any houses or other buildings? Can you see any animals, trees or other aspects of the landscape which shows you are not at home, in the time of your present body?

Turn to your right and see what lies on that side. Look at every possible thing because you will be able to remember it. Feel the air; is it summer or winter? What is the state of the vegetation, or are you inside a building? Is there any form of transport nearby? You will clearly remember every part of what you are seeing and sensing so now try to discover as much as you can about your environment.

Allow a pause of five to ten minutes, and unless anyone is looking restless or showing any other sign of stress, leave them to it. Even those who claimed not to have seen anything, unless they are obviously already bored by the whole experiment, should be allowed time to try and find out something new. You can ask each individual, after a suitable silence, if they wish to continue, or to return to the present day, or you might prefer to encourage them to remember a particular detail of the scene in their mind's eye so that they can return to it on a later occasion. Tell them to be very aware of how they actually feel, relaxed or tense, interested or weary, if they are enjoying the experiment or finding it hard to concentrate and so on. (This 'state report' can often help in later experiments because by recalling feelings and sensations, it is possible to mentally replicate these, and then return to that time or place on another occasion.)

Now it is time to return back to the old road and you will see there is a clear way for you to follow. You may walk slowly so that you perceive all the details of everything about you. Every part of the journey will remain clear in your mind as you return along the road through time. You will see that your steps are now on a smooth pavement, and the buildings are familiar. Gradually and gently you are returning to the door which you recognize as the one to this room. Slowly you will open your eyes and stretch, and before you discuss anything you will jot down some personal notes of your experiences and vision. Slowly, feeling quite safe and relaxed, you will return to be among us all here, in your own time.

There are many variations on this theme of a road or journey through time and it seems to work better than simply 'jumping back'. After a few attempts most people will begin to perceive, on one level or another, fragments of the 'other where or when'. Work slowly in this experiment, taking your own turn as a traveller, and allowing different people to narrate their version of the path through time. Learn from your group's experiences and make use of any helpful ideas which may come during any of the trips. Try to keep accurate and full records, even if you don't get clear pictures or details. These will come with practice. After all, it may well be a culture shock to discover your 'self' in another body, possibly of the opposite sex, in a distant time and place, playing a quite different role in a strange society.

How can you prove you are actually reliving a previous life and not just making it up, remembering the scenes from a vivid book or film, or simply deluding yourself on an ego trip? Well, you know yourself. If you remember a frightening moment in this life, what happens to you? How do you feel about the near or actual car accident, the serious illness, the death of a beloved? You ought to sense something in those situations which are physiologically detectable. The same applies to past life experiences. You 'feel' them just as you 'feel' fears or remembered pains in the present life. Try it and compare your reactions.

Clearly it will take many sessions before you begin to build up any great amount of information, but once you have discovered a way which opens the door to the past easily and effectively, gaining an entire collection of past life material is only a matter of perseverance. You will probably find that your memories are not neat and sequential and that you can't leave off at one point and then return during your next attempt to the experience which follows chronologically. Often you seem to hop between several different and sometimes widely separated lifetimes, seeing scenes from different phases of each, but following no obvious plan. The same could be said about memories in this life. What you remember about your childhood may well be scattered fragments covering ten or twelve years! When you are surveying the material gathered over any number of previous lives, the problem is decidedly greater. Patience is the only answer. Gather all the material you can, and try to reject anything which you know can be traced to a book or film, etc. The human memory has enormous capacity, and though it may not always be easy to gain access to its storage system, a lot of experiences are stashed away in there somewhere, not only from this life, but from many others, in most cases.

If you find yourself living before the 1500s traceable history becomes much harder to locate, being far more fragmentary and vague. This doesn't invalidate your recalled information, unless you are determined to convince a sceptic of the reality of reincarnation. This sort of experimental work is really for the magical student who wants to know himself in order to realize his entire potential, to develop new sources of ancient wisdom or to uncover the answers to those esoteric problems which are part of the Mysteries. Where and when was Atlantis? How did they build Stonehenge? For what purpose were the many 'burial' mounds and barrows actually constructed? Who was King Arthur and what did happen to Merlin? Do they still both sleep under some hill?

Maybe you will unravel some of these age-old mysteries, or produce the answer to the ultimate question. Perhaps you will write a series of fascinating books based on your earlier biographies, or provide information which conventional historians or archaeologists can confirm in due course. Maybe you were Napoleon or one of the Cleopatras, how does this knowledge benefit you in the twentieth century? More important, how does it benefit the rest of humanity? Karmic debts may still need to be repaid or old relationships worked through to a happy conclusion.

7.
THE MAGIC OF
SPACE TRAVEL

Today the idea of spacecraft visiting distant planets and space shots to explore the mantle of the sun are almost commonplace, and films and TV shows have made the universe seem quite small and close at hand. In the past such journeys, or even the notion that mankind would one day step upon the surface of the moon or planets was unthinkable, yet even in most ancient times magicians and wise folk have been able to project some aspect of their consciousness through space, and being invisible, witness events at considerable distances, or bring news of straying travellers to their families at the speed of thought.

There are really two aspects of this mental journeying and it is well worth the effort to make experiments in both types of 'space travel'. One is Divination, where by using symbols (such as the Tarot cards, the *I Ching* hexagrams or even a crystal ball) you are helping to focus your inner sight, clairvoyance or psychic vision on matters which may be occurring at a distance, or back or forward in time as well. Most often, this form of magical skill is applied to help or advise another person and so it carries a heavy responsibility. No one wants advice from a clairvoyant who is wrong! Also, if you give advice to other people, their lives may be shaped by your words, and you take on the responsibility for giving good and accurate assistance to them. If you should misjudge a situation you can bring unhappiness, distress or trouble to those you are aiming to help. It is a heavy burden, too often taken up without forethought or consideration of the implications of psychic counselling. If you tell folk what to do, you get involved in their karma, and webs of commitment and attachment are woven between you.

The other form of travel is often called 'Mindreach' or Astral travel, and in this case, although it may be used as a form of clairvoyance, it is more often carried out as experiments in which your awareness is projected out of the place where your body is resting so that you can perceive events at any distance, either nearby, or at any other point on planet Earth, or even out into space. It is a skill which may be developed from basic methods you should have learned already, like meditation and creative visualization. You may also be able to master the art by developing a pathworking which begins in your own home and ends in outer space.

Of course, there are many points which are common to both approaches and both require a lot of experimental work and practice. To learn the meaning of the symbols on each of the Tarot cards can be a lengthy enough business on its own, without adding to it the ability to change into that relaxed state of consciousness where pictures arise unbidden to expand the basic knowledge of each card's meaning within the spread. This is made harder by the presence of the person who has asked you to consult the cards on his behalf. It is much easier, within the still, clear atmosphere of the magical temple or special place, to allow the extra dimensions of information to flow through your awareness, than when you have someone sitting near you, concerned about the matter for which they have sought an answer. It is like the difference between trying to read a clearly printed book in your own language, and needing to decipher a note scribbled by a friend on a piece of newsprint which has accidentally gone through the laundry! When you are 'astral travelling' you may encounter similar problems.

Divination

Taking the matter of divination first, because it is something most students of occultism add to the repertoire of healing, ritual and meditation, there are lots of systems to choose from. Some use symbolic pictures or patterns from which information may be deduced: this covers not only the Tarot and the *I Ching* but also astrology, tea-leaf reading, the shape of an individual's handwriting and the lines on his palm. In each case interpretations of each card, hexagram, planet's position or line is combined with all the others in the divination, and from this much wider and more complex pattern, the future events, possibilities for the person's future or aspects of his character which he may have overlooked, can be developed and explained to him. It requires a lot of actual factual knowledge to recognize the significance of each of the seventy-eight Tarot cards, the sixty-four *I Ching* symbols, the ten planets/twelve signs/twelve houses and all the relevant aspects of a person's horoscope, or the possible variations of line, slope or pattern in someone's handwriting or palm. This body of information may be learned from a book, parrot-fashion, so that a beginner can chant 'Ten of Swords means complete disaster,' or 'Sun in Aries shows you're a bold, assertive, bad-tempered individual . . .' and so on, which will give little comfort to the person they are, in theory, trying to help!

There are plenty of recently written and genuinely helpful books on every possible sort of divination but words are not sufficient to convey what is actually encapsulated in every symbol of any system. This wisdom has to be achieved by study, thought and meditation. It cannot simply be read and remembered but has to come from within and it is experimentation which brings the deeper understanding. You will need to be able to expand the bare details learned from a writer whose words make sense to you, and whose approach to the divination system you have chosen agrees with your own general theory. Some of these may be scholarly, others light-hearted; some may be psychologically orientated, some personal or historical. In each case the way that you interpret the symbols as they have turned up in answer to some probably unexpressed question from your querent will vary with your own knowledge and the degree to which you are able to trust your own intuition in the matter. That, of course, is the key to an accurate and worthwhile reading. If your words only reflect some half-digested material gleaned from another's work it will not show you the clear pictures, words or other information which will help you pass on a good description of what may happen to your friend. You see, each divination symbol is really a reminder to you of some past event in your life/lives from which you can build a picture to convey to the person who needs your help. What actually happens to them won't be exactly the same as what you are remembering because that was a part of your own past, and the answer lies in their future.

The Tarot and the I Ching

In order to expand the amount of information you can extract from any card you will need to work with it. (There are card packs for divination with the Tarot and its many variants, the *I Ching*, recently the Phoenix Runes as well as the Celtic Tree alphabet, and you may well encounter others.) The most effective way is to have a small handy notebook and a new pack of your chosen cards. Shuffle the pack and place one card where you will see it. This need not be on an altar (although that is the best place), but a mantleshelf, on the kitchen wall, or even as a bookmark for when you are reading. Just allow any ideas, recollections or thoughts which are in any way evoked by that image to filter into your awareness, and then jot these down in your notebook. Take a new card each day until you have done them all and you will then find that simply to see any of the previous ones will immediately spark off a whole lot of information in your mind's eye. Later on you can add information gained from reading your chosen author upon that symbol. When you find the card in a future reading you will be able to draw a good word picture of it.

What will you be able to divine from such images, both on the cards and in your mind? Well, most querents will expect you to predict the future accurately. They will hope you can see the outcome of the situation they are in at present, and divine what factors will come into play in the days to come. You ought to be able to get a few details about the past of the individual or the events which have led up to the current difficulty, and even if you don't know what the exact problem is, this ought to be indicated by the first set of cards in the spread you are using, or in the initial hexagram of the *I Ching*. If the querent agrees that what you have said makes sense and relates to the problem he has in his head, or written on a slip of paper, or whatever method you use, then carry on. If the initial interpretation is way off mark, or doesn't make any sense, even to you, try again.

How does the above tie in with the concept of space travel and how can your methods of reading be made more clear and accurate? Well, when you are performing a divination for someone else their problem is not yours, and therefore it is at a distance from you. Whatever you discover will also happen at a distance or in the future of the other person, so in fact, this is a sort of mental space travel. In order to make it easier you should actually 'clear a space' in which you do the reading. You may well feel that you cannot put on full regalia and consecrate a circle as you would for any other ritual performance, unless (as is actually the best idea) you begin working with your magical companion on this art. If he or she is willing for you to learn to read the cards in answer to his or her future, or will perform a divination with the *I Ching* on your behalf, you can learn a great deal. You can also practise your consecrating skills, too, for any divination carried out within the mentally sterilized atmosphere of a magical temple or circle is much easier than one done in a crowded hall, surrounded by strangers. (Do bear this in mind if you have a reading done for you at an exhibition or garden fête!)

You will need to aim for a quiet atmosphere in which you can slip easily and gently into that altered state of awareness which comes from meditation and similar arts. You will be relaxed and unconcerned about ordinary events, but your mind will be clear, and whatever way information is given to you, it appears without effort as pictures, thoughts, symbols, flows of ideas or memories, so that it is easy to grasp and understand. With the Tarot it is necessary to have your eyes open to examine the cards, but you can then close them and allow images to appear. Relate these to your companion, who should write down what you say.

Crystal gazing
Another sort of divination you will need to experiment with is scrying. This is the art of crystal gazing or seeking pictures in a black mirror, a bowl of water or a pool of

black ink. In each case it is best tried within a consecrated circle which will banish those irritating psychic distractions which are present in everyday life. Allow yourself to sink into a relaxed state, perhaps at the suggestions of your companion, and then open your eyes to regard the crystal or other 'speculum' (scrying glass). Look within the glass, not at its surface and ignore any reflections of your face, or points of light that may be seen on its surface. Sink within it, forming a question in your mind to which you are seeking an answer. In a while, if you have reached the right level of distraction, you will find the glass seems to mist over, or become dim, and through the swirls of mist a dark patch may appear. You might find yourself sinking into this and then pictures, signs, numbers, words or anything may appear before you. This probably will not happen in the first experiments you perform, but if you continue for a number of regular sessions, allowing your companion to try in between times, you will gradually master this ancient and very valuable skill.

Palmistry and Astrology

Other forms of divination, which may involve predicting the future, include palmistry and astrology. In the first case, as in psychometry, (when you try to discover the history of an object, and thus details of its owner's life) you will be actually holding the hand of the person whose lines you are examining. Again learn this art with a friend, as holding hands with a stranger when you are in a receptive/perceptive mood can give a shock to the system – both yours and theirs! All kinds of impressions may flash through your mind's eye, almost too fast to grasp, and feelings, sensations and even strong emotions may flood over you from this extremely powerful symbol of their past. Speak aloud whatever you discover, trying to focus your companion's attention on one particular question, for example, as this will cut down the background 'noise'. Take each of the lines in turn and try to see what has happened in that field. Health and intellect may be quite easy but the heart or 'love' line may give you some vivid impressions to interpret. Looking for the future will involve holding and comparing both hands, seeing what physical changes show between the left (potential patterns in right-handed people) and the right hand which shows what your companion has made of his or her initial advantages in life, in all fields. The shape and feel of a hand will tell you a lot about the person, as will the colour, strength and depth of the marking indicate health and vigour. This works on an ordinary level, in that bitten nails and damaged quicks show a nervous disposition and lack of relaxation. As Sherlock Holmes knew, callouses and scars can indicate the sort of job a person does, for example. Don't ignore common sense when it comes to understanding the patterns in the lives of other people.

Modern works on psychology can provide a vast source of material about other people, and of course, yourself. Don't overlook anything which will make it easier to understand the workings of the human mind or the desires which motivate people to act. Simple introductory works on the theories of Carl Jung and other modern psychologists can provide valuable insight which can help you interpret a horoscope, read a palm, or divulge a character's secrets from a scribbled note. No one exactly fits the theoretical picture because people grow and change throughout their entire lives, and small-seeming experiences can change their attitude radically. Every divination is dealing with potential, both in the past and in the future. Not every potential musician takes up playing an instrument, any more than every healer is able to study medicine, yet now there are alternative applications of such talents, if they are discovered later in life.

To learn to travel through time for other people will require you to make some effort to understand what makes people tick, and learn the symbolism of whatever cards or other system you are using thoroughly, applying your own methods to expand and enhance that basic knowledge, probably gained from a book. You will need to practise being able to slip into a state of inner awareness where you can focus your attention on the past and future of the querent, and speak clearly of what you perceive. You will learn these arts within the quiet atmosphere of your magical circle with your regular occult companion, who can correct your visions, as you can assist him or her on experimental journeys through your past and future. Later on you may well be able to read the Tarot cards honestly and accurately, ignoring the crowds at a public show, or pick up clear and precise information about the future of a complete stranger when you take his hand at a party. This all comes with the application of concentration, study and regular practice. Any art will get easier the more you work at it, especially if you are able to control the circumstances in which you make your initial experiments, as within a magic circle or temple environment. This also applies to your first trips 'out of the body' or astral travelling.

Astral Travel

To some students, the ability to project consciousness beyond the place where you are physically situated is looked upon as the pinnacle of esoteric achievement, to others it is as common an activity as dreaming. In all probability, dreaming in some cases *is* astral projection. It is an art which most people, when they have mastered it, seem to find rather unexciting. Like other forms of altered states of awareness, the concentration is on the CONSCIOUSNESS, whether it be the ability to predict what will happen in the life of a friend, or to travel to the limits of the solar system just to see what it is like.

The methods to employ include some of those suggested in Chapter 6, Magical Experiments with Time. The traveller will need to be in a comfortable position, in a place where they can be quiet and undisturbed for a considerable length of time, have a companion who can take notes and control a tape recorder or provide paper and pencils for diagrams or sketches, and the odd snack at the conclusion of an experiment. Ideally you will need to achieve a state of physical relaxation in which you are willing to accept that some part of your consciousness can extract itself from your body and venture off through space, unseen. There is quite a mystique about the idea of projecting consciousness, and some of the methods suggested by previous authors seem extremely complicated or unnecessarily elaborate for something most people do when they are asleep!

You should always have a companion on your initial journeys as you will be deeply relaxed and the prospect of disturbances such as the telephone ringing or a visitor turning up at a critical moment can ruin your explorations, and can prevent you arriving at the precise sort of balance between your 'body awareness' and your ability to be aware somewhere else, on other occasions. One very simple experiment to try is to ask your companion to go into another room in your home and place some object in an otherwise clear space, where it won't be disturbed. Your experiment is to relax and sink into an altered state of consciousness wherein your ability to see or sense things can slip away from your body. Ask your friend to be quiet for, say five minutes, and then gently say your name and ask if you can 'see' the object in the other room. It takes a certain knack to be able to do this first time, but by meditating first and getting really 'switched off' you can often do it. Another experiment detailed in Targ and Puthoff's *Mind-reach* involved the traveller relaxing in a silent and controlled room whilst a laboratory technician drove for half an hour to another location. Then the astral traveller 'saw', as it were through the eyes of the other person, the location and its details which he then described in words on to tape, and in drawings or written description, after he had returned his awareness to his body. (It is possible to have dual consciousness, both of your body, and of the 'other location', as you will probably discover during your own experiments, but it is much easier to 'return' before trying to write, speak or otherwise communicate.) The laboratory technician in Targ's experiment, also wrote, drew and described his location, or took instant photographs etc. and then the reports from both were compared by a separate team of judges who had to decide if the place described seemed to be the same.

These experiments were first carried out with the best 'psychics' available but later tried with all sorts of people, including the lab cleaning ladies and some FBI agents who happened to want to know what was going on. (The spying potential of perfecting this method is fairly obvious as it is difficult to prevent astral visitors exploring secret sites as they are usually invisible and won't set off detecting equipment!) You can replicate the 'travelling through space' type of experiment by asking a friend to leave something on a table in his home, or by getting your regular magical companion to set up something for you to go and examine in another place. Later on, when you have both mastered the art you can both go to a special place and explore it, together.

One of the older magical methods of producing astral projection is by sitting in your temple and imagining yourself standing upright, preferably with your back to you, a couple of feet in front of you. Build up a strong picture of your own back, a pace away, exactly as you are dressed at the time (presumably in your magical robe), and try to see it, at least with your eyes closed. Remain as relaxed as you can and then transfer your awareness into your standing form. There is a certain art to this, which cannot be explained, but by experimenting you may well be able to get your awareness into the standing copy of yourself. This kind of astral 'cloning' has been known for a very long time, and seems to be illustrated on some old Egyptian papyri. When your awareness actually transfers from your seated, relaxed body into the image you have created you will suddenly find that you are looking at the room from that point of view. It can be a weird experience, and the surprise will almost certainly land you back into your body with a jolt, similar to that experienced when your body seems to 'fall' when you are going to sleep.

Auras

If your companion is able to see auras they might even see a faint figure building up in front of you, and your own auric field fading slightly, leaving the dense, inner 'etheric' or energy body around your seated form. On the subject of auras, there are basically three layers. The inner etheric is easily visible to ordinary eyesight in a dimly lit room as a smoky band about an inch wide outlining the figure, and is seen best against naked flesh. Beyond that is a wider band of the astral health region, seen as faint coloured filaments, such as you would see if you squint through your eyelashes at a candle flame. Outside that again is an even fainter layer, stretching away, of finer threads of the emotional aura, which connects to all the people, places and objects with which you have any link. Although there are numerous books on interpreting the colours of other people's auras, as to their state of health, moods and so on, you are never told that as you are looking through your own aura, the colours are a blend of yours and theirs! If the apparent colour is muddy and unpleasant it may not mean they are weighed down with ghastly karma, but that a combination of their colour and yours is not very pleasant. You can learn to see your own aura by standing naked in front of a large mirror in a dimly lit room, and squinting with your eyes unfocused, a few inches away from your reflection. The colours of the outer aura will be changing all the time, varying with emotion, hunger and temper, as well as general state of health, alertness and concentration on other people, which will brighten the filaments of auric material by which you are linked to them. It may well be that it is along these delicate threads the shared thoughts of telepathy may flow, and when you are psychometrizing an object, the impressions you receive are obtained from the same source. It is an enormous field of experimentation as yet unexplored for it will have valuable information to give about diagnoses of impending illnesses, mental depression or unstable relationships.

Archetypal Magical Temples

The most important magical aspect of being able to project your consciousness (with or without the astral body), is to be able to enter the archetypal magical temples. Each tradition of High Magic and of ancient Natural Magic has its sacred place. Some of these have a sort of history, like Atlantis or Avalon, or a genuine earthly base, like the ancient temples of the Nile in Egypt, each dedicated to its particular family of Gods and Goddesses, or our 'home grown' stone circles and sacred earthworks. Although these have some links with earth they are really only replicas of great sacred buildings or constructions which never existed as physical places. It is from these astral temples that power may flow into the small ritual rooms we construct to work in, and it is priests or powers which originate from these which convey most of the force we are able to raise in our workings. Magical tools, properly consecrated, become linked with their astral counterparts, as do robes and regalia, talismans and even people. It is through this contact with the 'Great Temple' that the most important and well established lodges draw not only magical forces for healing and esoteric workings, but great sources of knowledge and wisdom. Inspired teachings have their reality in an astral world, perhaps parallel to this one, yet invisible, like radio waves or television pictures, which constantly flow through us, undetected unless we have a receiver and aerial connected up. Here the great communicators or masters have their existence, and the 'Cosmic Civil Service' which seems to plan and direct the general pattern of certain individuals' lives on earth, have their offices. They are the ones who arrange those odd 'coincidences' which in retrospect prove to have been the most important meetings or events in our lives.

Your Reactions During Astral Travels

On astral journeys, as opposed to ordinary pathworkings, meditations or visualizations, you may find it hard to speak or indicate your impressions because you are not in your body, as you would be for these other experimental techniques. However, you should be able to recall the details later on and so give your companion any information regarding the object you went to visit, or the other location you explored. Your companion should also watch how you are reacting to your astral travels and may discover you look very relaxed and still. It is certainly worth while to have your companion suggest you can breathe normally, and speak, at the beginning of your adventure, and that if you make a movement of your right hand, for example, he or she should then gently call your name. You will be able to remember such keys to returning to your body.

If you use the 'building an astral form' method to get out you may be aware of a slender, silvery or rainbow-hued strand which seems to link your astral and your ordinary self, although it is not apparent to everyone. There are reports of it being joined at the navel, or the top of the head or heart area, so see if it is visible in your own case. The Bible says, 'If the silver cord is loosed or the golden bowl broken . . .' when talking about death, and it is thought that the silver cord is that which connects the astral or spiritual form to the physical, and the golden bowl is the aura, shown as a halo around the heads of

Christian saints and martyrs, though the size, density and colours will vary a lot, as explained before. If you find yourself in your astral form, floating through walls presents no trouble and you can fly, (as do many children in dreams, regretting that they can't do so during the day) and so visit distant places or scenes. You will learn to speed up your rate of progress by concentrating on the place you wish to visit. You can explore inside volcanoes and try skydiving without a parachute, but make sure you are on the astral plane first, and not actually about to leap out of a tenth floor window! When you want to return, see the place from where you set off and then re-enter the room. It can be extremely disconcerting to see yourself sitting quite still in your temple and this alone may well jolt you back into your physical aspect, but otherwise you will need to stand in front of yourself, and sink backwards into the seated position. Allow yourself a few moments to truely merge and become centred before leaping up and telling your companion all about your adventures. You will have been very relaxed for some considerable time and may feel a bit stiff or wobbly at first.

If you have succeeded in doing these exercises in the company of a friend you may try them alone, or in bed, projecting yourself up and out of your body, or as R. A. Monroe did, by rolling out of his body, sideways through a wall, as he explains in *Journeys Out of The Body*. It is possible to get into all sorts of weird situations, so do exercise common sense. It might seem to be fun to spy on people or 'overlook' someone you don't like, but they might actually see you! The astral police force, servants of the Great Temple, can also catch you at it, and if nothing else, limit your ability to do it at all, or any other work which involves the application of hidden knowledge.

Like time travelling, the more experience you have, especially when working with a trusted companion, the greater will be your self-confidence, which in turn will help you gain skills in all the other magical arts which are allied to travel, such as divination, scrying and clairvoyance. Gradually you will build up a link with one of the great teachers who will find ways of instructing you, often through those coincidental meetings or the sudden discovery of a book or other source of knowledge. You will be surprised what doors these experiments can open for you, if you persevere with them.

8.
MINDS OVER MAGIC

Most magical arts are very serious and require hard work and dedication. However, there is a diverse range of other 'supernatural' skills which you might never have considered. These can be valuable training techniques, or can even provide a variety of esoteric party games which your friends can play, and demonstrate their possible psychic talents. It is true that some people who have taken part in seances, played at 'raising ghosts' or light-heartedly dabbled with ouija boards and the like, have scared themselves, and opened doors to psychic perceptions which they did not know how to close, or attracted the attention of entities which they could not control, but if you are aspiring to master the skills of magic, you ought to know what you are doing.

The occult arts have always recognized the reality of the 'unseen' forces which may help and heal, instruct and guide. Magicians do not usually call up the spirits of dead people, accepting, on the whole, that the immortal human spirit needs to rest and assess its past life before being brought back into incarnation – it doesn't want goading by friends or relatives still alive into giving an account of its activities after it has cast off its mortal body. Nor will it necessarily have instantly gained profound wisdom, thus being able to answer all the questions which still beset those remaining in the 'vale of tears'. Certainly there are discarnate sources of knowledge which may be contacted through magical applications of some of the spiritualists' methods, but magicians generally prefer to use their own ways to receive information from hidden masters.

It is worth trying some experiments in Extra Sensory Perception, (ESP), Psychokinesis, (PK, affecting material objects by 'mind power'), and expanding psychic awareness. If you and your magical companion, or perhaps a slightly wider group of your friends and family, for example, can get together to try out skills like telepathy (conveying information from one mind to another), precognition or clairvoyance (guessing what card, for example, will be turned up next), or post- or retrocognition (listing the order of an already shuffled pack of cards). Scientists working in laboratories, with carefully selected subjects, using well tested methods under strictly controlled conditions, have made some progress in pinning down these elusive skills. In less formal tests it has been found that new subjects often score higher than those who had tried, and become bored, with card guessing, or attempts at bending metal. It was also found that a relaxed frame of mind, often difficult to achieve in a laboratory, was a help to 'travelling clairvoyance' (astral travel to the magician), and in tests in telepathy when one subject tried to 'see' the picture being looked at by a 'sender' in another room.

You may already have found that your magical interests have led to you getting 'hunches' about doing, or not doing, certain things, or that hints and clues are found in dreams, or that you actually perceive bits of the future clearly in meditations or during divination sessions. So long as you have control over your ability to use psychic faculties you won't get into trouble, but if you allow yourself to relax your guard and become frightened by your sudden clairvoyance, or power to seemingly affect and change the future, you will need to watch out. Don't play about with trances or try to contact 'spirits of the dead' as these can lead you into deep water, and if expert help is not to hand, can cause mental disturbance or depression. There are lots of safe and interesting experiments you can try and when you have fully mastered many of the psychic skills, then, if you are still interested, you may attempt more advanced journeys into the unknown regions.

Testing Your 'Supernatural' Skills
If you have a pack of Tarot cards or ordinary playing

cards you can begin some simple tests with your friends. Get someone to sort out the playing cards and then shuffle them very thoroughly. You then take this pack, face down, and picking the cards up one at a time, try to guess, imagine or 'see' what colour (or suit if you are using Tarot cards) each falls in. Place each card in turn on one of two or four heaps. If you get stuck with some cards make another heap, and go back to them at the end. You might be surprised how many you get right first go! Let your companion have a go and see if she does better or worse. You can even buy decks of special Zener cards which have five symbols on them. These are star, circle, square, wavy lines and cross, and they were invented to make scoring easier. If you make some of these cards you ought to score five out of the twenty-five cards right in any run through them by sheer chance. If you get six or more correct that is called a 'psi-hit' and is significant to investigators, especially if you can always score like this. If you always score less than five that is called 'psi-missing' and is just as significant. That proves that some aspect of your consciousness does see or guess what the cards are but deliberately makes you say or write down the wrong answer. To produce results which actually prove you are psychic may well take far more time and trouble than you are willing to devote to this experiment, but consistent significant scores do show you are waking up new areas of awareness.

An interesting methods (though it is sometimes harder to work out statistical scores), is to repeat the tests using a selection of picture postcards with clear images or designs. One person looks at the picture chosen at random from a selection and tries to convey the illustration to the receiver in another room. The receiver gets into a relaxed and meditative state, allowing his or her mind to be empty and tries to sense what is being seen. Although it is not easy to be able to draw exactly the same picture, receptive people (as all magicians ought to be) should get some aspect of the design, or indicate the feeling of the sender's mind. For example, if the card showed yachts sailing on a calm sea, with birds flying above, the receiver might draw triangles and say it felt windy, or sunny, or that he or she had a feeling of swaying, etc. Sometimes the emotion of a picture of lovers, or the scent of a flower, or the speed of racing cars can be sent more easily than the actual shapes, colours or minor details of the design. If possible, get a third party to match up the sender's and receiver's material, or allow the receiver to try and recognize the 'target' in a selection of cards. Again psi-missing can apply, shapes and colours being avoided!

You can use Tarot cards instead, and by sensing something of the meaning, even if it isn't an obvious tie-in with the scene shown on certain of the more elaborate decks, it may well link in with the symbolism of the card, either your own, or a more traditional interpretation. This 'game' has the added advantage of helping you form telepathic links with your partner, as well as possibly discovering deeper levels of meaning to the Tarot or any other system. Later on you may be able to send messages to each other at a distance, at first by trying to get your friend to recognize a colour which you send at one o' clock, for example, and by identifying a simple shape received from him or her at two o' clock. With practice, you might be able to send a number and a suit of playing or Tarot cards which would include a message, derived from the interpretation of that card or cards. Find out what sorts of information you can pass from mind to mind, starting with colours, plane shapes, numbers (either as the written figure, or a number of lines, dots or symbols, as that may be easier), feelings like energy, calm and so on. Use your own imagination to invent some suitable experiments to try. Each will help awaken, strengthen and control your psychic faculties.

Metal Bending

One subject which had a lot of coverage in the press and media a while ago was 'metal bending' and though some of the most famous demonstrators of this ability may have faded from public life, there are a number of eminent physicists in university laboratories still carrying out tests with both admitted experts and young people, to train them in this rather destructive and not very useful art. If you want to try for yourself you can resort to bits of cutlery, which were the things which made the headlines a few years ago, or strips of iron, steel or thick aluminium, if you come across any. You should simply relax into that useful mood of distraction, with the attitude, 'This is a game, it doesn't much matter if I succeed or not, but it would be fun to show that metal bending is possible'. Allow that sort of idea to flow through your head for a while, and then very lightly stroke part of the metal with one fingertip, whilst holding the bar gently with the other hand. Imagine it is a piece of plastic which can be sufficiently warmed by the heat in your finger to become soft and bendy. Even if you are just playing, don't exert any kind of bending force as this will invalidate your experiment, and prevent the 'psi-force' from working. Relax and imagine the metal doing the same. You may well be surprised after a few minutes to discover a slight bend in the bar - or possibly not! Certainly metal can be bent by forces as yet not fully understood by physicists, and far more people can develop the ability if they really want to, but it doesn't have many peaceful applications. Try it for fun, and if you succeed and want to demonstrate your skill to the experts, find one of the serious books on the subject, and write to the author, care of the publisher. You might find an outlet for your new found skill on television!

Psychokinesis

Although the above application of PK is not very useful and you may not have that many spare spoons and forks, you might like to try some other tests which show the same forces in a more entertaining and less destructive manner. One way to find out if you can move things by will power, apart from sitting staring at a ping-pong ball on a tray, out of draughts, and willing it to move, is to obtain a Crooke's Radiometer. You may have seen these at shows or in shop windows. They are glass spheres, about four inches across, and inside is a pair of fine wires, balanced on a pointed pivot. At the end of each arm is a small diamond shape, coloured white on one side, and black on the other. The whole thing is sealed in a vacuum. The Radiometer will remain quite still in darkness or dim light, but if the sun, or even a candle, shines upon it the white sides will reflect the heat and the black sides absorb it, and so untouched by human hands, it will slowly begin to turn clockwise. Your task is to make it go the opposite way by will power. You may not thump the table, and blowing will not help as the unit is sealed, but some people can actually make it go round the wrong way by psi.

A simpler set-up you can make yourself consists of a slender straw or grass stem attached to the finest hair or strand of a terylene thread and hung from the lid of a screw-top jar. At each end of the straw a vertically mounted circle of coloured paper is attached forming 'paddles'. This should be able to turn easily within the container, which should be sealed so that the air within may become totally still and any natural twisting movement left in the supporting strand can unwind. The whole set-up should be placed on a totally firm and stable bench and you will see that any slight movement of the table, floor or even house might be enough to cause the bar with its paddles to turn. Once you have allowed the apparatus to become absolutely still after a day or so, without touching the jar or table, begin to 'will' the bar to turn on its spider thin thread.

Poltergeist Activity

You may already have noticed a psi force at work in your home which makes objects move without any obvious touch or jarring. Of course, if you live near a main road, railway, underground line or airport your whole house is likely to shake a bit. Even factories which use heavy machinery can have a subtle effect on places at a considerable distance, depending on the soil type in the area. If things do seem to move about, or vanish, or even strange items suddenly appear, it means there is a psi force operating in your home. This may emanate from you, as a result of your magical practices, or it could be the energy field of a young person. Many teenagers do develop this strange flood of energy, usually between the ages of about ten and fifteen. Quite dramatic poltergeist activities have been recorded with furniture flying about, noises in the night, the telephone going mad, and electrical equipment turning on and off without being touched. This energy never does any harm to anyone, but it can be terrifying for those involved. However, once you pay attention to the youngsters and allow them to let off steam with games or outings, by sharing their emotions and guiding them during this critical stage of growing up, these phenomena soon vanish. They don't require exorcism nor the intervention of priests, merely loving care, time and the release of tension and zest through normal activities like sport, dancing or drama.

Ouija-boards

Many people, who do feel they are under psychic attack, have done something to open a door to some of the playful energy which lurks about in the unseen world which flows through us. Often they have tried raising spirits, played with a ouija-board or held seances, without having any real idea how to go about it safely.

Like any experiment with unseen forces, whether magical or psychic, you will be working with altered states of awareness. In magic you, as the magician, are trained to be in control – in playing with ouija-boards and the like, this is usually not the case. When a few people sit in the light of a guttering candle around a table, circled with the letters of the alphabet, with quivering fingers placed on the stem of an upturned wineglass, it is no wonder that everyone is keyed up for a visitation. Very soon, if the tension and expectancy is sufficient, the glass will begin to move. Will it spell out 'death' or 'I am the spirit of the devil' or any other such common comment? Possibly, and everyone will get very excited or scared, depending on their nature. Perhaps the glass will zoom across the table, or jerkily start to spell out messages from the departed. Tension among the participants increases, and doubts and queries arise in their minds. 'Is there some spirit moving the pointer?' 'Yes' the glass will answer, or 'No' if it is in that sort of mood. Sometimes clear messages are laboriously spelled out, or else there seems to be a great force causing the glass to jerk violently from letter to letter, trailing garbled words or plain nonsense. Whatever happens, everyone taking part will have had a weird experience which they will find curiously hard to forget. It can prey on the minds of unhappy people and cause them to have strange dreams and become unsettled so that any out of the ordinary happening takes on a great importance, and they become very frightened. Often, because their awareness has been sharpened by this slight brush with the unseen, they convince themselves they are under psychic attack when they break a favourite ornament, and that the itches of gnat bites are some imps sent to torment them. It really does happen!

If you get invited to join in such a game do make it clear to the others that it is not the best sort of activity to dabble with and that the consequences can be far reaching. When the glass does spell messages these are almost always derived from the subconscious of one or other of the participants, or from the collective unconscious mind if it is a well established group. Because people expect to get messages from dead relatives, that is the form the words may well take. If they expect to feel cold or clammy, sense touches or hear knocks and thumps, the chances are that they will. The same applies to table-turning or tilting, when a circle of people sit with their hands lightly on the surface with little fingers and thumbs just touching. After a while, in the dim red light, after the singing of some eerie hymns or prayers, the table will seem to move, sway and even tap out letters. The slightest nudge will set it off on its erratic course through the alphabet, or even careering about the room with the disturbed sitters in hot pursuit. This is an extremely slow and clumsy way of getting divine instructions or communicating with the discarnate masters, and magicians will soon find that safer, quieter methods of meditation and contemplation provide far more reliable sources of information, than cracking glasses or breaking the legs off tables!

Unidentified Flying Objects
Although magicians may have individual views on the subjects of unidentified flying objects (UFOs), and may not personally have seen that many ghosts, they accept as a part of their mystical heritage, the reality of elemental spirits of nature, and the fairies of past times, as well as the giants and heroes of myth and legend. It may not be immediately obvious that there are definite links between all these different sorts of visitors. Recent surveys have indicated that many UFO sightings appear over ancient sacred sites; fairies or elves are often seen at crossroads;

ghosts haunt churchyards (or staircases), and elementals can be found in wild places. Most of these are 'places between worlds' or 'set apart'. Churches are often built on much older pagan sacred places; crossroads were frequently locations of meetings of witches, and fairy folk will turn up anywhere where nature has enough energy to support their existence. Most of these beings exist primarily on another plane and come into our set of dimensions where the veil is thin and the separated worlds meet. In many cases these places have always been sacred, weird or set apart. Usually they have rocks beneath them which are crystalline, radioactive or have some other property which our ancestors recognized as a power source, and made use of when constructing circles, standing stones or earthworks.

The art of shape-shifting has been attributed in turn to witches, angels, fairies and the occupants of flying saucers. It wouldn't be too great a leap of the imagination to say that all these creatures have certain things in common, if, in fact, they are not indeed the same. They turn up at the same sort of places, seem to be able to draw on energy supplies which well up from the earth, and even those who might have originated in spacecraft from the other side of the galaxy tend to appear close to the ground, hovering, glowing and leaving little or no trace of their visit. It seems extremely strange that extra-terrestrials come all the way to earth and then vanish without saying 'Hallo'! If they are wiser, more advanced and so on, which they must be to have got this far successfully, it is a shame that they don't leave a calling card. Even the people who are invited aboard their craft do not receive a souvenir of that momentous visit to show their earthly friends.

In Biblical time spacecraft didn't exist so it was 'Chariots of Fire' and flaming wheels; today we have intergalactic spaceships and science fiction films showing ETs and Vogons. In the Middle Ages only angels flew through the air and, apart from the odd saint, human beings stayed safely on the ground. Today flying faster than the speed of sound is commonplace, and trips to the moon frequent, at least by man-made research craft. However, we still have our share of fairies, elementals and ghosts, appearing where they always have done, as recorded in local tales and legends, but now they may appear as space travellers, and their balls of light as UFOs. One curious fact about these visitors is that if something is seen by a psychic person, he can draw the attention of his non-psychic friend to that object or creature, who can then see it too. Now, that is a piece of magic!

There are undoubtedly forces around ancient sites, be they what scientists can measure and record as ultrasonic pulses, high frequency radio waves or energy surges which appear as shape-shifting balls of light in the sky, and are seen as UFOs, angels, etc., depending on the psychology of the viewer, rather than the actual object. Magicians may not need to give these forces technical names, but they ought to learn to detect them, by dowsing with rods or a pendulum, or actually by feeling the power in a standing stone when sitting relaxed against it, or by discovering the bands of energy with their hands. It is this force, which can be detected in the ley lines, that seems to link ancient sacred sites, standing stones, mounds, moats, marker cairns, notches in ridges and groves in a vast web of energy. Whether this was created by the wise ones of old, or whether they detected its force and wove the strands between certain places is not yet known, but gradually its secrets are being uncovered and the Gordian knot of this antique power source is being unravelled by those with the width of understanding to delve into it. Maybe, in the future, the power for peace on earth can be fed into the network, to flow through all the places where war and hatred rage, calming and stilling the anger and restoring peace and prosperity. Let healing, love, justice and plenty flow through the decayed veins of Mother Earth and all her children may benefit from this power, once they learn to recognize it.

Psychic Healing Power

You can apply psychic forces to healing in a variety of ways, healing not only people, but animals, trees and perhaps the very Earth herself. One of the simplest things to do is to get some fresh spring water, preferably from a healing spring, and then bless it in the name of the God or Goddess of Healing. This can be a Christian saint or simply 'Lady of Health' as you wish. Place your hands

around the container for a few moments and then experiment with the 'holy' water on things like potted plants or
even seeds. Compare a pot of seedlings sprinkled with the
consecrated water with a similar pot given only tap water
– you could be very surprised at the difference. This water
may also be added to a bath, for relaxation and healing,
or given to ailing animals or children, as well as to any
friends who wish to share your experiments. Aches and
bruises may be bathed with this healing water, and sickly
trees or shrubs, even in public parks, may well benefit
from a dose of blessed spring water. You might find your
healing power is such that each time it rains you can stand
in a doorway or under a tree and bless the rain as it falls, to
bring healing and fertility to the land, and all that grows
there.

You might also apply your psychic healing power
through consecrated oil. Take a little almond or 'baby' oil
and bless it, and use this as a healing balm for sunburn,
itches and to enrich your hands and feet before a ritual.
Offer your magical companion samples of blessed and
untouched oil and see if she is able to detect the difference.
If you have done the consecration correctly and brought
down the power of healing into it, you will be able to
detect a difference in temperature, or a feeling of glowing
or some other sensation. The same is true when you bless
a humble candle before a ritual, or consecrate a talisman.
To the psychic senses it will feel very different. Experiment
with something as ordinary as a pair of postcards of the
same picture. Bless one and not the other and see what
the difference is.

If you can't sense it with your left hand, or by looking
with your inner eye, maybe a pendulum will help. Ask 'Is
this the consecrated item?' over each in turn and see
which it indicates as positive. Learn to get it right.
Dowsing is a very simple art, and anyone can soon get a
pendulum, made of any small, symmetrical object, like a
bead or plumb-bob on a thin thread, to give a definite
positive swing and a clear negative swing, which will be
easy to tell apart, even if they don't comply with the
patterns of swing given in a book. It is your inner
awareness which is helping the pendulum to swing, and it
will react as it chooses. Check each time that it is being

consistent, then you can add another game to your psychic repertoire.

Playing 'Hunt the Thimble' may sound a bit childish, but if you go about it as a training exercise, or as yet another in a series of experiments you and your companion can try to expand your awareness of your unexploited talents in the psychic field. With a pendulum in one hand use the other as a pointer, after your friend has hidden a 'thimble', which is best if it is something like a significant lump of rock, or a consecrated object as it is easier to find. Point around the room and watch for the pendulum to change from swinging idly to a positive movement, and then gradually move nearer to the place it seems to indicate by cross referencing until you locate it. Again it takes both practice and confidence in your inner sight to be able to see through walls or under cushions to locate a hidden, or later on, lost item.

Until you gain expertise it is worth playing a few games with a pendulum – this is one of the subtler skills you can teach children too. Hide a coin under a loose carpet and let them take turns in dowsing for its location. Help them trace water pipes or cables under the lawn in the garden, or, indoors, blindfolded, follow the courses of rivers or the sea coast on large maps. Get samples of as many metals as you can and hide each under an upturned cup and award a small prize for the person who gets the most right. Ask 'Is this silver?' over each cup in turn, or brass, stone, copper, glass or plastic and see how expert you and your companion are getting.

When you do have confidence you may use the pendulum in healing, not only as a way of diagnosing the seat of an illness, but also as a radionics tool for creating a healing potion. Again, using spring water, or the basic milk-sugar tablets used by homoeopaths to make their medicines (available from natural chemists), you can create a useful therapy. With a clipping of hair, a signature or some other 'witness' of a sick person placed under the container of water/pills, hold your pendulum over it and say 'Make this a medicine to cure so-and-so's illness'. You will find it will begin to swing in large circles over the medicine and continue for some time, gradually slowing down and finally stopping. This has then made radionically (the art of using dowsing for diagnosis and healing, or other methods which use the same underlying principles) a potion which the sick person should take each day, for a whole moon, starting as soon as possible. Note whether the moon is full, new, waxing or waning, and see how the patient progresses during the next four weeks. You can even hold the pendulum over the person, if they are willing to try this unusual form of healing!

Experiment with Psychic Forces

If you are certain you have psychic powers (which most people possess though they haven't all bothered to learn about or train them) you can make a 'poltergeists' playpen' which is, in fact, a miniature laboratory, combining a number of experiments for these loose psychic forces to interact with, inside a sealed container. If you can get an old aquarium, or even a large sweet jar with a lid from a shop you can develop a number of things which the forces may use. You will need some kind of striped or squared paper to make a background so that even tiny movements of objects will be apparent. Some stationers sell large squared sheets, or even fancy wrapping paper with a chequer-board pattern might be available. Stick this firmly to the longest side of the tank/jar. On the floor you will need to spread a light powder which will show when objects have been moved. This could be talcum powder or flour, or even instant coffee powder. You will need to make little swings as suggested on page 112, suspended from the thinnest thread, and provide a ping-pong ball or other light object which might be moved or rolled about. It is worth putting in a heavy stone or lump of wood in case there are very strong forces wishing to demonstrate their power. Get a couple of interlinked metal rings which are soldered so they won't simply unlock, and a dice to discover if it will roll on its own. All these things will need to be placed inside the 'lab' and then it will have to be sealed, perhaps even getting the lid glued or fastened with a small padlock so that no tiny human fingers can get in among the playthings.

The 'lab' will need to be placed on an immovable support, for example on top of a wardrobe, and well away from anyone or anything which can physically jar, shake or affect it, if the experiment is to have any validity at all. Set it up, and allow each item to take up its natural position. In a few days, as long as nothing has obviously interfered with its resting state, you can begin to call upon any psychic forces which happen to be around to enter this esoteric funfair and try the equipment provided. It may take ages before anything noticeable happens, but you may find that there are tracks of movement in the dust, or that the trapeze has turned round, or even that closely sealed interlinked rings have unlocked – or that unlinked solid rings somehow defied logic by interlocking. Springs might be found straightened out and unbent pieces of wire curled into patterns. No one knows what these forces are, but they do seem willing to play in such equipment, and if you get results, please let me know. In many universities and laboratories all over the world technicians are striving to evolve suitable tests which will demonstrate the sorts of powers magicians take for granted.

9.
THE ARTS OF TALISMANIC MAGIC

Amulets, charms, spells and talismans are all used in various books dealing with magical arts and often it is not made clear precisely what is being inferred, so it is important to start off with some sort of definition of these various artefacts.

Amulets
Amulets are an extremely ancient form of PROTECTION, especially against the 'evil eye' and are often made to represent an eye, or are natural stones, pieces of wood or pottery in that shape. In ancient Egypt the symbol was called 'The Eye of Horus' and was drawn like the natural black lines of feathers around the eye of an Egyptian falcon, whose head was often used for that of the young sun god. The shape, which some modern magicians believe represents the inner parts of a human brain, the seat of esoteric power, is still found on modern medical prescriptions as ℞ which is taken from the Latin word 'recipe' meaning 'take thou . . .' Amulets ward off harm by drawing the glance of the ill wisher to the carved imitation eye rather than to the real eyes of the victim so that the evil intent may not land and enter his soul through the gateway of his eyes.

Charms
Charms may be natural objects which are intended to bring luck or ward off other sorts of evil intent. They may also be chants or simple rhymes which are intended to dispel a problem, like warts, or protect the charm bearer or singer from a specific sort of harm. Many of the oldest

charms are derived from nature, often being fossils or naturally occurring crystals. As our ancestors had no clear understanding of what caused fossils to be formed these were looked upon as strange works of the Gods. Some were lucky and would attract health and others were the harbingers of misfortune or sickness. The good stones included ones with holes in, for these were hung over the doors of byres and stables to prevent the animals being attacked by spirits in the night, when they would be ridden to exhaustion, or milked dry. It was believed that evil sprites would try to get through the holes in the stones and become trapped, so that every seven years the stones had to be thrown into running water and new ones found. Usually these stones were tied with red ribbons as the colour of life. These 'holey', holy or Hag stones turn up all over the country and in Europe. Other almost perfectly spherical holey stones are actually fossil sponges which vary in size from that of a pea to that of a walnut and they were sought by witches who made them into necklaces. They also make excellent magical dowsing pendulums.

Fossil ammonites curled like snakes, were believed to ward off the poison of snake bite, and those found in Ireland were thought to be the snakes which St Patrick had turned to stone when he rid that green island of its venomous serpents. Belemnites, bullet shaped fossils derived from some kind of squid or sea creature, often turned up by the ploughshare, were called 'elf bolts' and were supposed to have been shot to inflict harm on children or cattle. Similarly, ancient flint arrowheads made by Stone Age people, were looked upon as harbingers of evil, and unless ceremonially cast into running water or buried deep, they too might bring sickness or ill luck.

Spoken or sung charms were usually used to drive away sickness and were often doggerel rhymes, made up to suit the person for whom they were intended. A simple, but still effective wart charm may be said as follows:

Wart, wart, black of heart, I command thee to depart.
As our Lady Moon do wane, be he free of spot and blain.

Usually there were fairly elaborate instructions to be followed in that each wart had to be counted and a leaf picked from a sacred tree for every one. These leaves were buried, thrown into water or even impaled upon the thorns of a May Tree, or perhaps the sap from a dandelion was smeared on each wart to show it up black, or a piece of meat or a snail was rubbed on every blemish, and in turn impaled, buried or drowned, depending on the local theories. Many of these ancient charms do literally 'work like a charm', but be careful if you start experimenting with spells using creatures, even those as lowly as snails and slugs.

Some of the well-known children's nursery rhymes were originally charms against the plague. For example, 'Ring a ring o' roses, pocket full of posies, atishoo, atishoo, all fall down' was hoped to keep away the miasmas which caused pneumonic plague, as were the scented posies of herbs mentioned in the rhyme. There is a vast mine of information scattered among these old rhymes and folk songs which have preserved for hundreds of years both magical charms and valuable pieces of myth and legend, upon which the work of modern occult groups is ultimately rooted. The common country folk were wise far beyond the educated, book learning of the town folk and religious orders. They preserved in folk song, ditty, spell and symbol, a great deal of very old knowledge, which, because it retained its virtue even in the face of science, has in some part come down to us today. Much is still to be rediscovered from these sources of knowledge and practical crafts.

Spells
Spells are again the application of the spoken word. In the days of the Druids, their Bards could win battles by singing satires against the leader of the opposing army, revealing the secret names of their Gods and the weaknesses of character of the leader. The voice or the musical note, used correctly in magic, is a very powerful instrument. Spells may be woven to enchant and entrance by hypnotically repeated phrase, both the singer, if he is a shaman, or the hearer, who may be lulled into a peaceful sleep in sickness, or incited to riot and fight by the battle hymn of the blood chant. The stamp of the foot, beat of a drum or jangle of the sistrum in the hands of true priests can

invoke in the hearers all kinds of powerful emotions and actions. Pop music can do the same by inflaming the fans in wild adoration, and the shouts of the military junta can lead the mob into slaughter and pillage. Trained occultists are aware of the forces which sounds can call up and use their voices with care when calling upon the sacred names of their God and Goddess.

Experimenting with Sound

The old books of magic hint at the 'unspeakable names of God'. These aren't so much unspeakable but unpronounceable. Most of the old alphabets did not have vowel sounds as we know them so a combination of consonants might be spoken in a variety of ways, as the letters 'tn' could become 'tan', 'ten', 'tin', 'ton' and 'tun', each with a different meaning. Expand the word to more than three letters and it becomes vastly more complex. In some systems it is the vowel sounds themselves, which pronounced alone, invoke power. One way to experiment with this is to find a place where a bit of noise will be tolerated, under a railway arch, or in an empty bathroom where there is some echo, and by dropping your voice to a lower note than that used for ordinary speech, vibrate the letters A, E I, O and U. The results will certainly surprise you if no one has shown you the trick before. With practice, you can get your whole body apparently vibrating in harmony, once you have hit the correct pitch. When you then invoke the words of power during a ritual it will have a great deal more effect. Vibrating sounds need not be very loud; you aren't aiming to shout at God, but to send out a powerful call which will resonate on the other levels of existence. You will need to do some breathing exercises, so experiment with whistling and deep breathing to increase the power of your lungs and the length of time you can vibrate any note. Work with your companion too, for he or she will resonate to a different note and you ought to be able to harmonize so that when invoking together you have an even more devastating effect.

Another technique which is worth learning is the use of chanting or humming as a way of releasing tension. You can teach this to children too, because they often like to shriek and scream, unknowingly for this very reason. Start off by groaning low and loud, putting into it all the held in feelings of disappointment, despair and unhappiness you can actually manage. A whole roomful of people doing this is an amazing sound! Groan and moan out all the mental pain and repression you can, and as you feel the burden of it slipping from your mind, let the sound rise in pitch, gently and gradually, so that after a few minutes you are beginning to sing, on any note which pleases you. Try small runs of notes or scales, in any mode or key, until you find a simple tune forming, which you may hum or sing. Perhaps a single note seems totally satisfying to you, or you wish to change pitch and add rhythm until you have made a tune. If you are with other people you may well end up singing in harmony, and you will feel much better for the exercise.

As you develop a pattern of ritual with prayers, invocations and chants you will see how music or vibration of certain words will add a new dimension to your working. You can chant a simple spell each day for health, based on Coué's theme, 'Every day, in every way, I am getting better and better!' – a much safer tranquillizer than some of the chemicals on the market! You may like to learn a musical instrument or find recordings of either classical or modern tunes which fit the theme of your rituals, meditations or pathworkings. You may well be able to fill in gaps of silence with background 'musak' as there is a good deal of meditation music available now. Experiment with all kinds of sounds; drums, bells, gongs and flutes have all been used to add to the atmosphere of religious and magical ritual through the centuries, and even the addition of single dings on a pleasant sounding bell can add effect to the simplest ritual.

Talismans

When you come to the making of talismans, the most complex art of this kind, you will need not only the words to say for the consecration, but the elements with which to bless the completed work, as well as the skill, equipment and materials to design an effective talisman in the first place. Each one is a specific magical charm designed for one person, to work on one occasion, so you can't make a batch of 'good luck talismans' despite the claims made about such items that you can buy through the post! Every talisman has to be made for a particular person and situation and you can't practise or have test runs, any more than you can have complete rehearsals of magical rites!

Talismans require several sorts of information and skill and should not be undertaken until you are competent at the basic arts of visualization and human psychology. Anyone who makes a magical charm, with the application of intent and will is responsible for the outcome, for it forms very strong karmic links, so do think first before showing off this aspect of your magical know-how. You will need to know the correspondences of planet, colour, number, God/Goddess names, gems, plane figures and astrological information relating to each talisman and all the people involved. It is always best that you and your partner start off by working on your own behalf so that you can observe what happens during the making, consecrating and finally the working of the talisman. You will need a genuine reason to launch this difficult branch of magic, not just a trumped up excuse to play with clay and coloured pens.

As well as knowing on what day and at what hour the work should be done you will need to assemble material for the talisman, either the correct planetary metal (gold is a bit pricey, so gold foil or paper will probably have to do, for example), and inks to write on it. You will need a connecting link to the person it is intended for: hair, a signature or photograph, etc. and some silk or fine cloth of the right colour to make a cover for it. You might need clay or wood, jewels and sewing thread, felt-tip pens and parchment, metal foil or particular gums for the incense sacred to the powers whose influence is to be woven into the talisman. These items may well not be to hand, unless you are already a competent magical jackdaw, hoarding all the necessary bits and pieces. You may well also need to learn certain practical arts, like calligraphy, astrology, metal engraving, poker-work, embroidery or herbalism, in order that you have the necessary skill to make, consecrate and empower the talisman in a way that will ensure its success.

Magical Correspondences

The most obvious set of magical correspondences which will cover most of the situations you will meet to begin with are those associated with the days of the week. You should know the planets from the names of the days: Monday – Moon; Tuesday – Mars (Tiw, Saxon or Mardi in French); Wednesday – Mercury (Wotan, Saxon); Thursday – Jupiter (Thor, Saxon); Friday – Venus (Freya, Saxon); Saturday – Saturn, and Sunday – Sun. Each of these planets, astrologically speaking, has certain associations with influences, colours, incenses, flowers, and so on. You will need to research the underlying symbolism and arrive at a set of correspondences, which even if they don't agree with anyone else's, satisfy you and your magical partner. Don't rush this research, it is a part of making a talisman, which is a much longer process than scribbling a brief spell on a bit of paper and wrapping it in green paper! From the moment you decide to make a working you are already involved in the process, and it will not be completed until the aim for which you are working has been accomplished.

Often there are several forces whose help is needed to complete the work and these must be understood and balanced so that each is given its due. For example, a talisman to get a specific job would involve Jupiter (business), the Sun (for yourself), and Saturn (because you want a particular job concerning the Law or old people). If you are trying to interfere in the lives of other people – DON'T! Do not make 'love spells' or potions, because whether or not they work you will have created unnatural and lasting links between people and have interfered with their destiny. You cannot see the outcome of any relationship, nor what is planned for each individual to achieve, so don't meddle. If someone asks for this kind of help you can assist them to attract a suitable partner or lover but only by AFFECTING THEMSELVES, not some other person, no matter how good the argument seems to be. You will only win love, affection and respect if you are WORTHY of these feelings, not because you have bespelled and lured the affections of someone who you may heartily dislike once you have got together! Earn love by being lovable and by giving out warmth and compassion to all those around you; it is the strongest and safest love potion in the world

Making the Talisman

You will need to establish the colour, materials, day and God forms related to the subject of your talisman and gradually gather such equipment as you need in order to make it. You can simply manufacture the charm and then consecrate it, but as you are experimenting with different techniques, actually making it magically can teach you a lot. After checking the correct items are assembled on the right day, you and your partner can enter a kind of shared litany of question and answer which adds enormously to the power of the completed talisman. When you begin, for example, with your piece of new parchment, cut accurately to a square (for a Jupiter talisman), and take up a blue pen to write upon it she asks 'Who is this talisman to be made for?' and you answer. She then asks 'Is it with his/her will?' and go on, after your replies each time to enquire 'Why that shape?' 'Why that colour?' 'What words/symbols/jewels/metals are you using?' 'What is the purpose of the talisman?' and 'By what right do you set this plan in motion?'

If you are genuinely sharing the work, she should also be allowed to have a part in making the talisman, and then you can ask her how it is to be consecrated, why a particular incense is being used, how the cover which has also been made will help to retain its power, and so on. By doing this you will both learn a great deal, especially if the questions are prepared by each of you and not asked before the work begins. When you have ensured that the work is complete, that the talisman states its purpose and is linked both with the person for whom it is made, and with the god/power which will bring its intent to fruition. If it is for yourself you can link it by writing your magical name or motto on it, signing it, or by adding a drop of your blood or saliva. Even so, it should be completed by both of you and finally sealed in a bag or wrapping of new cloth (silk is far the best) of an appropriate colour, and bound with a different coloured thread, perhaps plaited from the number of strands to correspond with one of the factors involved. The final parcel should be carried around with you close to your heart, if its purpose is knowledge, health, or some on-going matter. If you want a bit of specific luck, a new job or home then it is best to place the completed talisman, when it has been consecrated, under your bed, out of the way, until one moon, or three signs of the zodiac have passed.

Consecrating the Talisman

When the practical part of making the talisman is complete, you still need to consecrate it. This need not be on the same day, for example something with both the Sun and Venus involved, such as a talisman to bring success to a growing partnership, could be made on a Sunday and consecrated on the following Friday, or vice versa. This will also need preparation as you will need the elements of earth, water, fire and air in the form used in your ordinary rituals, and if the talisman has been made of wood, metal or clay (which may need to be fired and glazed, possibly, before consecration) you will need some holy oil. This is usually made from almond or olive oil to which herbs, gums, resins or chips of wood from the tree dedicated to the planets concerned is added. This is left in the sun for a while so that the essential oils and perfumes may suffuse the oil. You can buy it ready made and appropriate to any planet or power, but it is much better to make your own for magical purposes. It can also be used to dedicate people at initiation or degree ceremonies, if these should fall within the compass of your activities, in due course.

You will need to set up the temple, with the altar in the centre and next to the altar lamp the newly-made talisman and its cover. When you have blessed each other and sealed the circle you should sit opposite each other across the altar. If that isn't possible due to lack of space, try to make an equal-sided triangle with the altar and your seats as this gives power to the working, as does the first position suggested. Don't rush through the words or the actions as it takes time for the powers to build and the help you are asking to come and enter the talisman. Using words like:

Lord (or Lady) of Air (*Fire, Water and Earth, in turn*), bless this thy symbol, and let power be indwelling.

Go round all the symbols, and if possible carry them to each point of the compass, or elevate them in the right direction. Share this work between you because this is both conscrating the area and the items themselves, which in turn, you will use for empowering the talisman. Each holding one hand over the oil say your own version of:

> Great Lady/Lord (*name of planet or other force you wish to infuse into the talisman*), enter into this oil, that it may bless and dedicate this symbol and give it the power to work effectively in this plane of Earth.

If you each normally work with two of the elements it is a very effective way of first cleansing the new talisman of your own influences by, in turn saying:

> Spirit that moveth on the face of the waters, wash from this symbol all past associations that it may be pure and dedicated to its new purpose.

One of you should say the words whilst the other sprinkles a few drops of water on the talisman, using a twig of the appropriate plant if you know which one is dedicated to the planetary force you are using. Then the other one sprinkles a little salt upon it and you say:

> Lady of Earth, foundation of our lives and work, take away the links of the past, and instil into this talisman the strength and stability that it may perform its true destiny.

Try not to actually touch the talisman after it has been cleansed unless it was made specifically for you. Lift it on a cloth or piece of cardboard or slide it into its cover, at the end of the ritual, using a wand or dagger.

You still need to circle it with fire, which as the energizing element will begin to make it come alive. If you can't pass it through the lamp flame, that is if the talisman is made of paper or cloth, circle the lamp about it. The same applies to the incense smoke, which as a representation of the 'Breath of God' will blow life into the talisman, so that it is fully effective. Work out an invocation which mentions this, so that you can put into the talisman all your feelings about it. You can even have another set of questions and answers which explain to the

the talisman, so that it is fully effective. Work out an invocation which mentions this, so that you can put into the talisman all your feelings about it. You can even have another set of questions and answers which explain to the powers you are calling upon what the talisman is intended to accomplish, who it is for, and so on.

You may like to sit in silent meditation or even listen to some appropriate music for a few moments to allow any energies to spiral into the new talisman before you complete the work by 'switching it on' with the holy oil. When you are ready, both dip your forefinger into a little of the oil, placed on a small dish on the altar. Imagine there being a pool of light which you can transfer on to the talisman. You will need to find some powerful words to exactly express your intention for the charm. Together say firmly, as you touch the oil onto it,

'In the Name of . . . I consecrate this talisman of . . .'

Wait for a moment as it may be that a surge of energy is actually felt or the incense smoke will swirl or you will perceive light flowing around the new talisman. Carefully slide it into the cover which should be fastened securely. Then share a cup of wine and bread if that is a usual part of your ceremony. Do not hurry, just because it seems you have completed the work. Gently unwind the circle, put the equipment away, disrobe and slowly come back to earth. Leave the talisman on the altar before the centre lamp for as long as you can.

This may not seem a very powerful ritual, but if you carefully choose words and actions and research the correspondences of the planets and so on, you will be surprised what forces you are able to see or feel when you complete the work. The entire ritual is roughed out for you as writing all the words and actions of any ceremony can take away a great deal of its power. If you work through the chapters of this book you will find all that you need to master most of the arts of a really competent magician, in your own style. The experiments here are meant as a guide so that you can find your own individual path through the Mysteries, which you would not get if the whole of a ritual system, used and developed by other people, was simply set out before you. By making up your own ceremonies on a conventional framework you will discover a far more potent system, exactly suited to your own needs and abilities, than merely copying, parrot-fashion, someone else's work. Be patient and you will grow in knowledge and understanding.

Other Magical Charms

You will find lots of information on traditional charms and amulets in books of folklore. Some lucky stones are large, like the Men-an-Tol, the 'stone with a hole' on the Cornish moors which has a legend about people who crawl through it. Many similar stones or nooks and crannies in cromlechs and dolmens were set up to represent the womb of the Earth Mother, and by ritually crawling through the hole a candidate became a 'Child of the Earth Goddess' and one of the twice born, or initiates. Horse-shoes, so long associated not only with the mysterious, magical crafts of the smith, were symbols of the Horse Goddess, called Epona by the Romans. She is the great ancient image carved on White Horse Hill, near Uffington. Nearby is the long barrow called Wayland's Smithy, a site of ritual and initiation, still filled with power. Both these, and their associated sites, lie close to the ancient Ridgeway path, which is almost literally, as old as the hills. Along it there are many places where luck or magic might be sought, and where gatherings of folk were held, to work the magic which makes the corn spring green each year, and the ewes bring forth twin lambs.

Many ancient earth works and settings of stones map out great talismans on the very face of the earth; certain stones act as 'acupuncture needles' bringing healing and certain energies, either from the sky to the earth, or from the inner earth to those who walk on her surface. There are numerous healing springs or wells which are famous for their magical associations, and lots of places where traditional ceremonies are held, even now, to bring fertility, luck or success to the surrounding lands. Fire festivals in Sussex echo the bonfires of Hallowe'en, and burning 'guys' and setting off fireworks were common activities before the Gunpowder plot in 1605. Burning ships in Shetland at January's 'Up Helly Aa' is reflected in the flames of the Rye bonfire in November. These are all genuine spells to ensure harvests of fish or field or to burn out ill luck or sickness. So when you are trying to decide how to tackle a small personal problem, remember that such arts were used on a far greater scale in times past, and that your experiments are only repeats of things wise folk have been doing for thousands of years, all over the world. Museums are full of ancient curses scratched on lead (the metal of Saturn, Lord of the Underworld) or of cuneiform inscriptions which are medical or magical spells. Corn dollies are charms in which the spirit of the Corn King lives out the winter. Seashells, fossils and strange shaped stones ward off harm, or attract success. You are certain to find some magical charms in your local museum, during traditional festivals celebrated in your own area, or where you may go on holiday, not only in Britain, of course!

10.
GODS FOR THE FUTURE

Most of the previous experiments have fairly obviously been concerned with some aspect or other of magic, but how can you experiment with religion or your relationship with God, or even with a total disbelief in any supernatural agency? You will probably have been brought up with the tenets of some orthodox faith, accepting perhaps 'God the Father', 'Thou shalt have no Gods before me . . .', 'there is no God beside Allah, and Mohammed is his prophet . . .' and 'God, the Father, Son and Holy Ghost'. You may have been taught about the Virgin Mary, or having taken to pagan ways have learned of the Earth Goddess or Mother Nature. As a magician you will have to examine the concept of the male and female sides of deity, the God within, and the idea put forward by Dion Fortune, in several of her books, 'All Gods are One God, and All Goddesses are One Goddess, and there is One Initiator'.

A magician does not have faith; he is not taught to believe, but just as he gradually becomes aware of his powers to change events by the logical application of his magical intent, he will have EXPERIENCE of God and the Gods during his work. Most conventional religions make the point that God is unknowable, being too great and complex for mere humans to grasp in totality. This has led to the introduction of hierarchies of priests, bishops and the like, and even modern witch covens have High Priests and High Priestesses. In each case these priests may set up a barrier between the seeker of God and some aspect, at least, of Deity. It is possible to come to terms with the idea, as Dion Fortune has done, that there may be many gods and goddesses, just as there are many planets and stars whose influence is apparent in any horoscope, but that there is a Creator/Initiator/Primal Stream from which comes the energy of change. Qabalists may talk of the 'Logos', Biblical scholars of 'the Word'; Skywalkers of the 'Force', and you may discover some other term which seems absolutely right and totally descriptive for your own experience of Deity.

In working magic it is necessary to understand that the power you use to alter events, effect healings, and bring about the accomplishment of your magical intention, need not only be directly contacted and that there may be other ways in which you can communicate, but that by interacting with this power, a strong link may be formed. This is a link of personal, direct experience. You KNOW your prayers can be answered from first hand experience. You may read that within you there is a spark of the Divinity. You will gradually discover that this is both male and female and is much greater than simply being of a neutral spiritual nature.

Many people, in the last few decades, have expressed their dissatisfaction with the Christian church and have sought other paths to spiritual fulfilment. Some have taken the seemingly easy path of agnosticism, denying deity, and then wonder why their spells have no power or effect. Many have been led along the oriental ways of Zen and Buddhism, meditating on the goal of samadhi and total detachment. In the Middle Ages there were a large number of sects which separated creation into two sections, matter and spirit. Matter was ruled by Rex Mundi, the King of the World whose image still appears on the Tarot trump of the Devil. The Cathars, the Albigensians and many other similar groups maintained that God was a spirit and could not live in the flesh, and so Jesus the Nazarene was a prophet and preacher but because he lived and died on earth, could not be God. They were the keepers of great secrets, one of which might have been the Holy Grail. This is usually thought of as a cup or cauldron, according to the Christian or pagan sources, but it was described as a stone or as a secret, perhaps not material at all, which could be perceived in some special manner by the chosen few.

The Shroud of Turin

Research is unravelling bits of the story of Jesus, and even after 2,000 years new material is coming to light about his life, work and death and either survival or resurrection. The Shroud of Turin may hold some vital clues as to the state of the body around which it was wrapped, in antiquity. If carbon dating tests are finally permitted to demonstrate its age, it will provide a very interesting piece of evidence for religious detectives. Maybe the body was still alive when placed in the shroud, although in a state of deep trance, similar to that often recorded by fakirs and holy men in India, who were buried alive, in lead coffins, sometimes for months, and yet came forth alive and well at the end. If Jesus had studied with the Essenes, or any other ancient mystery school, he may well have learned the arts of suspended animation. Being nailed to a cross for only a few hours would hardly kill a man in his prime, and in good health. Felons were hung until eaten by birds yet Jesus was taken down and reverently laid in a cave tomb, where, in some of the New Testament accounts, two white robed 'angelic' figures attended him. Were these healer priests from his own order who stood by after this extreme sort of initiation test to ensure the candidate survived, as did the Sioux warriors when candidates suffered the ordeals of the flesh hooks?

No one really knows if Jesus existed, how closely his life fitted any of the stories, which themselves are extremely varied, in the New Testament. None of this information was written down at the time, and it has been much edited, changed and influenced by the views of the different people whose hands it passed through. Much has been omitted too. Perhaps he did survive the crucifixion, and married Mary Magdalene, as has been suggested. Maybe he continued his travels with Joseph of Arimathea, who legend reports, brought him as a child to Cornwall or Glastonbury, or both. He may have lived many years after recovering from his ordeal of 'birth/death/rebirth' on the cross, and the blood of his children may well live today among the powerful families all over Europe. When they find his body and match it with the Turin Shroud and openly reveal all the ancient texts which deal with his life, ministry and message it may be one far closer to the hearts of many people than some watered down religions seem to be.

Paganism

People turned to paganism as a way to escape the formal dogma of the orthodox religions, but in some cases cast off one set of beliefs for another equally alien one. It is pointless, spiritually, to deny the value of the Church and then bow down to some self-appointed priest who still acts as a go-between, separating the Gods and the people. Religion is a matter of personal experience and should not need to be mediated by anyone. You will have to decide how you can think of the Creative force which set the path of evolution going, and which seemingly, still has some effect upon living things. You must decide if you are happy worshipping a Goddess who may be, in fact, the very earth beneath your feet, or Mother Nature, invisible yet living in every plant, animal, tree and stone. You might like to work with the image of Isis, so beautifully described at the end of *The Golden Ass*, a book of initiation and mystery written in the second century of the Christian era by Apuleius. The pagan Goddess is symbolized by the shifting pattern of the moon's face and she usually has three names, Maiden, Mother and Crone, and different attributes for each phase. In the calendar of the pagan year each of the nine main festivals celebrates some aspect of the life story of the Goddess of Nature/the Earth/The Moon and her Son/Consort/Lord whose symbol is the Sun, whose growing and fading strength is echoed in the part he plays in the rites. Many of the ancient festivals have modern counterparts and the old sacred dances, for example, are still performed by Morris men.

Many of the ancient sites have religious as well as calendar associations. The vast hill figures are both depictions of aspects of the Gods of Old and clearly seen gathering places where folk came to share their feast days and work their magic. Cerne Abbas has its vast virile giant as does Wilmington in Sussex, although he is only seen in outline these days. The great white mare who is also a dragon, showing the association of the powers of inner earth with the serpent or dragon force of the whole planet, is still the focus of magical workings. Remember, if you wish to celebrate your rituals at some ancient sacred site you do not have to be there physically. No one can stop visitors photographing, not only onto film, but into the library of the inner vision, all the details of such important places as Avebury, Stonehenge, the White Horse, Arbor Low, the Rings of Callenish and the Avenues of Carnac. Look at these places, absorb their atmosphere and you will learn that you can recall it in great detail at home, in the quietness of your own temple.

You must come to understand that spark of God/ Goddess within you so that its voice can advise, its power can direct and its influence help you grow in all the fields which you are capable of mastering. YOU can be the greatest in the world, if you first discover in which area you wish to excel, and by cultivating skills guided by that inner contact, you alone can help yourself to succeed. You may also find ways of encountering each sort of God and Goddess you have ever heard of. The most effective way of meeting the Dieties for yourself is by steeping yourself in the legends or mythology of any given era. Don't mix these up. Isis won't appreciate being called up in the company of Wotan, nor Lakshmi with Cernunnos. Start with the Gods of your own people, because their symbols, sacred places and tales will be closest to you. This is not easy, but then nothing worth doing ever is. Suddenly you will find the flat pictures in some book or the patterns of stones in a field near you come alive, and you will become aware of great presences with whom you can communicate.

The Four Elements
Many of the books on paganism and witchcraft insist upon superhuman type figures for the God and Goddesses, but this does not appeal to everyone trying to escape from the images of the orthodox faiths. There is no reason why you cannot envisage the powers as abstract forces or energies and interact with them accordingly. The most powerful magical system, no matter what it may be called by its followers, still relies on a special relationship between the magician and the four elements, Earth, Water, Fire and Air. Many lodges work with these forces

in the form of the Archangels: Auriel, or Uriel, is generally associated with Earth and clad in robes of the colours of Malkuth, black, olive, citrine and russet; Gabriel is the Blue-robed archangel of Water, and healing; Michael, dressed in armour of flaming red and gold and bearing the great sword is an angel of fire and Raphael in airy golden robes guards the quarter of Air. These aren't gods, but great forces traditionally personified as taller than life figures, stationed at the four points of the compass. In the witch's circle the elements are offered in salutation at each quarter in turn at the opening and closing of the ritual and there the Lords of the Watchtowers (derived from the works of Dr Dee in the sixteenth century), are requested to surround the working. Traditional witches raise a castle within which time is stopped, and in many other ceremonies some sort of representations of Earth, Water, Fire and Air are placed about the circle or on the altar. Again these are not specifically related to gods or goddesses, although they may be given the names of pagan deities in some groups.

You may feel happier working with forces that are symbolized by the four elements, by the male/white/positive pillar and the female/black/negative pillar. A few sessions of meditation on this dichotomy is very worthwhile and it may well uncover aspects of deities about which you had not previously thought. Remember, dark and light are not good and evil! You cannot have up without down, left without right. Everyone should strive to be in a state of balance and equilibrium. If you are convinced that the insistence on 'God the Father' has to be couterbalanced by 'Goddess the Mother' alone, you will swing the pendulum just as far in the other direction. The world needs stability of God/Goddess, Father/Mother, Day/Night and Summer/Winter. Even the Bible, using the term 'Elohim' implies male and female deities.

Do not simply reject all previous religious upbringing and turn to some neo-pagan rituals just because it seems a good move. Within every sort of faith there are keys to the mysteries, and even the Christian message was for the few and not the many. 'Love thy neighbour as thyself' only makes sense if you are willing to love yourself, not in a selfish way, but by truly understanding who you are and where you are going. You are the standpoint by which you judge the rest of the world, and the closer you are able to get to perfection, the better is the whole of humanity. If you become part of a group and have to accept different Gods and Goddesses to those you have encountered before, meditate upon them, in the forms in which your group works with them. Get to know them and any stories or legends associated with them. Many of the Gods and Goddesses may have been human heroes once, or, like the Gods and Goddesses of Classical Rome and Greece, each had a specific job or association and these characteristics were linked with one of the travelling stars which we know now to be planets.

The Need to Worship

Dr Carl Jung became convinced that as well as a need for food, shelter, love and security, mankind needed to worship something. In modern times many people worship a pop-star, a football team or even a possession like a car or house, rather than a God or Goddess. It is because people have reduced this innate longing to such mundane levels that they are feeling cut off and disconcerted about their lives. We are living in an age of great changes, but then the human race has almost always been in times of change, ever since the discovery of fire. Instead of living, as the farming folk did for hundreds of years, knowing their successes or failures were in the hands of God or the gods, people seem to have come to rely totally on the State for their well-being, housing and other needs. Some have cast off the responsibility for almost every aspect of their health, occupation and situation. Now it is time for every aspiring magician, at least, to examine his or her feelings about religion, God, the Gods and Goddesses of pagan times, and maybe even discover new deities for the new age.

If you really are drawn to the Lord of the Wild Hunt and the Great Earth Mother you will not be able to encounter them in your ordinary home, unless you live in a cottage in the middle of Dartmoor. You will have to make a modern pilgrimage to a wild place, to sit in the depths of a winter wood, or a summer moor, where cloud shadows chase across the purple green hillsides. You will have to cast off the mode of thinking of the town or city and allow your deeper, wilder nature to come to the surface so that you can feel the presences of the Great Ones. You may see them as vast figures looming across the sky, or feel the breath of the Lady on a spring wind, filled with the scent of primroses or hawthorn. You might begin to realize that the whole globe of the earth is actually a living, sentient being, the goddess Gaia or Ge, and that you are living as a creature upon her mantle. You may begin to realize how the earth has been spoiled and how greed has begun to destroy the very foundation upon which we live. You will have to go through some strong feelings if you open up one of the doors to this sort of religious experience. It might even lead you to the way of the shaman, who abandons awareness for the ecstasy of unity with the Goddess who inspires him. This is very different from the groups of modern witches who dance around in a candle-lit basement with artificial flowers, and images of the Goddess in glo-lite plastic!

To embrace the Old Ones honestly will require a great deal of dedication and change in your life. Whether you are initiated by some one with superior knowledge, or if you choose the lonely path of the solo-seeker who becomes one with the Great Goddess, to be reborn her child, you will be changed. You cannot remain the same person. Your view of life, modern motivations and personal objectives will change because she has blessed you; or because you have genuinely encountered the Lord of the Wild Things, you can no longer feel safe among man-made walls. Material possessions and mundane security will no longer seem important, and your whole outlook will be radically changed if you dare to take this path to the wilderness.

If you cannot commit yourself to being truly pagan you may take the softer option of reawakening the contacts with the Classical Gods of Rome, Egypt and Greece. Their stories are well documented. Many of their temples or sacred places are still to be seen, and in some of the more remote ones, the power still lingers, or can still be perceived by those who know how to open their inner vision. You may be able to build something of the surroundings at home in your own temple, but your need to experience these ancient sacred sanctuaries first hand for the contact which will make their gods apparent to you. Once you have absorbed as much of these places as you can, you can develop pathworkings which lead you to the innermost inner, where the classical Gods and Goddesses had their dwelling. Begin by simply setting the scene, and allowing the vision to build up, and you may well be surprised how strongly the pictures before your inner eye develop and become 'real'. If you and your partner have both visited the same places you can take it in turn to create scenes from the relevant temple or grove and as you become more expert the pictures will unfold before you so that you can report them to each other.

The Gods and Goddesses need the worship and contact with humans just as we need their help and inspiration. By allowing their will to work on earth they are strengthened to perform greater miracles, in conjunction with their followers. Everyone who serves the classical Gods or is united and reborn into the family of the Great Ones is in some way helping them to accomplish their wills for mankind. We are all a part of the whole, be it cosmos or universe, or even thoughts in the mind of the Creator. 'God created mankind in his imagination, male and female created he them . . .' We must try not to forget this very important fact.

Working with Ritual

When you begin to build up elaborate rituals you will probably become aware that when you consecrate the elements you are making a change, not perhaps physically visible, but just as a good priest at mass symbolically changes the bread and wine into the body and blood of Christ, so are you changing mundane objects into spiritual ones. They become 'of the Gods' by the blessing of those Gods whose aid you invoke. You may wish to make some of your rituals entirely religious, either by celebrating the traditional feasts or by making your working a method of speaking with or observing the Gods of your chosen system. Here you will either need to go to the wild places to meet the Great Ones who are reluctant to come to cities and towns, or you will need to create the images of the Temples of the Nile, the heights of Olympus or the

Standing Stones of some British sacred site. To do this is an inspiring activity and, like most magical acts, it is the performance and the resulting experiences, which are the real secrets of magic, and will prove whether or not you have actually made a contact with your deities.

As well as celebrating the many festivals you might choose to work with the Moon Goddess in her threefold form, as Maid, Mother and Crone, and use her power for each aspect to help with your work. She will bring magical inspiration if you dare to allow her mystic influences to seep through your inner being. This is another form of dedication which must be without reservation. You cannot command the Gods, you can only try to align yourself with the associations traditionally linked with them and allow the magic to work through you. This requires courage and commitment and cannot be simply withdrawn if you discover a new hobby. Magic and initiation are forever, no matter how feebly they are done in the first place. If your intention was to serve the Great Ones (even if the coven or lodge you joined proved to be a bunch of amateurs) it will be taken as such and you can't just back out!

Observe how the God of the Sun and the Lady of the Moon affect your waking and sleeping life. See how the tides of the year, separated by the solar solstices and equinoxes, change your feelings and magical abilities. See what each phase of the moon does to your dreams and visions and you will soon learn how strongly the bonds with the God and Goddess have been forged. Experiment with different sorts of religious activities. Try pathworking to the sacred places, experiment with conjuring visions of the deities you choose to work with. Consecrate and bless things in their name and see how their influences change ordinary items into magically powerful instruments. Make up ceremonies of thanksgiving - not only for ordinary help received, but for all the good things in life - butterflies, beautiful flowers, strange animals and wild places. Get into the habit of talking to your Gods and Goddesses as if they were invisible friends. Imagine they are part of your family, as you have become a part of theirs. Get to know them and all the symbols associated with them. Discover their feast days and what sort of offerings of grain, flowers or incenses were prepared for them. You cannot sacrifice life to the Creator or any of the Great Ones because they gave it in the first place; you can only offer yourself and any work you may do on their behalf.

Prayer

At the end of each ceremony close with prayers or poems of thanksgiving and praise. Ask for peace, for harmony in the world, love to overcome hatred and health to conquer disease. Think not only of your own land and people, but of the sufferers in other places, those without any of the things which you take for granted – clean water, shelter, help in sickness and relief from poverty. There is enough for all and the world can be made into the paradise it is meant to be by the properly applied magic of prayer. This is the force which works unseen and causes changes at an inner level, allowing power to flow outwards bringing benefits and changes for the good of all. Illness is cured from within, in a sick person, either by his own will helping him to regain the balance of true health, or by the medicines which he has taken assisting in the healing process. This is also true of the whole galaxy. Ask that the Great Ones bring peace and true understanding and somehow those in high places will become inspired with thoughts of peace. You would never be able to change their minds by argument or brute force, but by the subtle application of the seeds of wisdom sown by people of goodwill, and tended by the ancient Gods on the inner, all things may be brought to change.

Prayer doesn't have to be performed on a certain day each week, in a particular building. The influence of the Great Ones is all round you wherever you are, and they will listen to your words and hopes at any time. You do not need priests to guide you or intercede for you. If you have sinned then the laws of karma will show you how reparation may be made. Muttering a grudging prayer to the Lady Mary will not necessarily relieve your feeling of guilt, nor will it help whoever you have wronged. Punishing the body will not affect the soul and confession to someone as human as you simply shares the burden, it doesn't relieve it. You will have to consider the matter of wrongdoing and forgiveness in the light of your understanding of your original religion and that of the deities you now choose to worship. Again, this is a personal matter which you should work out for yourself.

There are a couple of other points about becoming a working magician or witch. If you feel that you are able to become a mediator of the power of a particular God or Goddess you must recognize that you must become worthy. There is nothing less pleasant than encountering some egocentric High Priestess who believes she can call down the power of Isis, yet has not the humanity to get on with her fellow coven members and treats them like dirt. If you want to become the vehicle of the Great Ones you must not only strive to become worthy in your everyday life as well as magical life, but you must recognize the responsibility that such an act entails. You can't play at being Isis, Horus, Cernunnos or Artemis without understanding what that involves. You can only really be the servants of the Old Ones, trying to do their will and work on earth. If they choose to temporarily dwell within you it is a great honour and a heavy burden.

The same responsibility rests with people who take the names of Gods and Goddesses as their magical names. If you can live up to the onerous task of being the Goddess of Wisdom or the Lord of Travel and Thievery all the time, well and good. If you are really only a simple human being striving to master the arts of magic, then calling yourself 'Servant of Saturn' or 'Child of Isis' is infinitely safer!

The Path of Unity
Everyone is a child of earth, each of us can look up at the sky and know that without the power of the sun we would have no being. From this simple notion you can build up an important relationship between yourself, the created world and all the other inhabitants. Many people on drug trips have experienced a feeling of oneness with all creation; others, who have studied long and hard in the Eastern yogic traditions hold such unity as an objective. In the West it was the shamans and priests of the old ways who so involved themselves with the patterns of the earth

and sky that they became absorbed into the oneness and unified with creation. This can happen to you. There is no sure way of going about this dissolution into the infinite, but it is a goal to aim for if you accept that we are in fact parts of a greater whole, but cut off by false beliefs and separated by having forgotten our roots. As with all other magical acts, you need to be in control and not under the influence of drugs or any other person. The path of Unity is a lonely one, and will cut you off from many of the human contacts with which you are familiar. That path will set you apart and change your views of modern life even more radically than true initiation might. It is not an easy way to travel, and there are no signposts and few fellow travellers on that strange way. You alone can choose to set out on that journey, for it is another experiment, but if you feel it is your way, what you learn upon it could help all creatures understand their unity and involvement with one another's plight.

Do examine the religious ways of other people, read their books and experiment with the tenets of their faith, for though you may reject much of it underneath many different religions lie the same ideas and aims, most of which should make sense to a modern magician. Soon we may be living away from earth, and having to discover a new set of sacred places and acts of worship to suit the space age, yet the new ideas will have been grown from the seeds of the old. Perhaps research in archaeology and science will uncover material on which the major faiths are based, and radically change them into a belief for the coming age. Maybe a new Messiah will emerge, or the old one come back for a rerun! Perhaps people will realize that all of them have the spark of the Divine within them and do not need outside Gods or priests. If they can understand the nature of the human spirit, both male and female, which lies within the core of every individual and make this a life-giving force for healing, creativity and contentment many of the long held hopes for the future of mankind on earth will be achieved.

As a magician you will need to discover by experiment your own true feelings about God, the Gods and Goddesses, the Creator and the invisible, unknowable power which exists within everything from the tiniest microbe to the greatest universe. To change one part of that creation is in some way to change the whole. If you make changes by magic you hold the whole responsibility for what happens to the entire cosmos. It is an awesome concept, but magic is an awesome undertaking, not for those of weak will, nor feeble intention. Every ritual is an experiment, and can never be exactly repeated.

Another aspect of religious experimentation is in the keeping of a shrine. Britain is dotted with ancient sacred sites, springs, groves, hills, tumuli, stone circles and prehistoric settlements, all of which may well have had their priests, priestesses and oracles in times gone by. You may be drawn to explore such a place near you, clearing away rubbish, planting bulbs or flowering plants and making it a good place to visit. Some traditional holy sanctuaries are well known and visited by thousands of people each year, others have been long forgotten, but their sacredness and the wisdom stored in their stones is still there to be reawoken by a devotee. It is in this way that the highest form of worship and magical aspiration can be drawn down to the earth, and links between the forces which govern the whole cosmos and us below may be strengthened. Even a small corner of your room can become a dwelling place of the Gods and Goddesses, or the Creator, if you wish.

It has become clear during the last few years that ancient sources of knowledge and wisdom are once again being opened to us, if we treat them with reverence and respect. From the oldest sacred places in the land to the newest location of the inspired seer, drops of the elixir from the Cauldron of Inspiration are pouring into our world of consciousness. Used correctly this information can go a long way towards rebalancing the forces for peace, for love and for eternal justice in our world, so long as the new venturers into the paths of magic do not take it upon themselves to preach, to indoctrinate or to pressurize other people to follow their personal vision. The magic of worship, calling on the Great Ones for help or guidance and healing is something between you and them, shared only by your working partner or group. If you have a clear vision of the Gods, angels or powers that is a special thing which should be kept private and respected. Converting the masses to yet another faith or promulgating your inner vision will not lead those who have not found the way for themselves one step nearer their own destiny. The message will come from within as a direct revelation, it cannot be enforced from outside, as history so clearly demonstrates.

Magic is not a light undertaking, especially as it works in all aspects of your life and no one can be absolutely certain of the outcome of any act of magic. It is always an adventure, a journey into the unknown regions of your inner experience so venture with care and forethought. Adhere to the ancient adage 'To know, to will, to dare and to keep silent' and you will find that the Gods guide your travel and the Lady will keep you safe in her care.

CONCLUSION

Magic is a vast subject. Even the study of its history can take a lifetime. Every magician will be making a new path through the various traditions, selecting the symbol systems and God forms which most closely match their own aspirations. From the simplest rites of the Natural magicians to the most complex and elaborate ceremonies of advanced Qabalist adepts, each will have researched, experimented and discovered a way which satisfies their magical will. It is a matter of personal choice which you will have to make for yourself.

Today there are plenty of new books written by competent practitioners of every possible path, both Eastern and Western, simple or complicated, religious or dedicated to the service of creation. If you have been able to use this book as it was intended you will have experimented with a number of techniques, compared theory with practice and explored areas which you may never have dreamed were parts of the work of the occultist. Your work will never be finished for in magic, as in life, you never cease to learn new things and undergo new experiences.

Perhaps you had been hoping this book would reveal all the secrets of magic for the dawning age of Aquarius – in fact, it has. The secrets of magic are concerned with experience. Unless you are willing to try the various arts suggested here, or work through the methods of the ritual magician or the festivals of the modern witch, the secrets remain secrets. YOU will have to experiment, sometimes facing the hard lesson of failure, which teaches you a great deal more than the success which seems to be a 'fluke'.

You will learn how to shift your awareness to a level when meditations, pathworkings and visualizations create the images and then the reality which you are seeking. No one can do that for you, nor can reading every book published demonstrate to you the power to heal, the curious coincidences which bring about your magical will, if you will not exchange your armchair for your temple throne.

A new magic is being created now, suitable for the people of the end of the twentieth century. Gradually, like a tree growing the first leaves are spreading so that we can begin to recognize its nature and perhaps its ultimate form. At present we do not know how tall it may grow, nor what its flowers or fruit may be – these may take years to develop fully. But everyone who is willing to make the experiments here, in the attitude of exploration and wonder, all manner of things may be revealed to you. It will be your work which will help to unlock the secrets of the Gods for the future, the magic arts and skills which you learn and practise may assist those who follow in your footsteps. Our lives are so much changed from the simple ways of the first magicians who watched the stars and speculated on their powers and effects upon the earth. They left us no books to read, nor videos to watch yet somehow, within such artefacts which have come down to us is enshrined a great store of wisdom. It is up to us, using our will, consciousness and inner perceptions to discover how this knowledge may be recovered. Already many alternatives are seeping into everyday life – in healing, alternative therapies, often based on ancient natural methods, are being made more readily available; in entertainment all sorts of options are to be tried; in food and drink natural and untreated produce is being sold or grown at home. We have the option to live as slaves within a system which we cannot alter, or to take destiny into our hands, through the application of our trained magical wills and so bring knowledge, healing and peace to all about us.

When the circle of those wise in the hidden ways of magic can join hands around the great circle of the earth, and gather in the greater circle of the skies, then surely the will of the Gods for mankind upon earth will come into being and a new and magical future will open before us. Take up your courage, your common sense and your sense of humour, fasten these within the magical sphere of your trained attention and set off into the unknown that you may bring back a light to guide those who walk behind you. There is a blessing on all who serve.

FURTHER READING

Ashcroft-Nowicki, Dolores, *First Steps in Ritual* (Aquarian Press, 1982).
— , *The Shining Paths* (Aquarian Press, 1983).
Glaskin, G. M., *Windows of the Mind* (Arrow paperbacks).
Hope, Murry, *Practical Techniques of Psychic Self-Defence* (Aquarian Press, 1983).
Green, Marian, *Magic for the Aquarian Age* (Aquarian Press, 1983).
Jung, C. G., *Man and His Symbols* (Pan, 1978).
— , *Memories, Dreams, Reflections* (Collins, 1983).
Knight, Gareth, *The Secret Tradition in Arthurian Legend* (Aquarian Press, 1984).
Matthews, J. and C., *The Western Way* (Arkana Paperbacks, 1985).
Stewart, R. J., *The Underworld Initiation* (Aquarian Press, 1985).
Toffler, Alvin, *The Third Wave* (Pan, 1981).

SULIS MUSIC produces cassette tapes of magical meditations by Marian Green, Dolores Ashcroft-Nowicki and R. J. Stewart. List available from SULIS MUSIC, BM Box 3721, London WC1N 3XX.

FURTHER INFORMATION

There are dozens of small magazines, local suppliers and booksellers, both in shops and by mail order, but because these change their address, close down, or merge with other similar businesses, it is not possible to give a comprehensive list. The most enduring of these dealers are listed below and *Prediction* magazine, published monthly and available from any newsagent, frequently advertises publications, training schools, suppliers of incenses and so on.

ATLANTIS BOOKSHOP, 49A Museum Street, London WC1 deals in most current books.

THE SERVANTS OF THE LIGHT ASSOCIATION, PO Box 215, St Helier, Jersey run a postal course of instruction based on the works of W. E. Butler and Gareth Knight, and publishes *Round Merlin's Table* quarterly.

DUSTY MILLER AND SON makes all the wands, rods, charms and symbols of the Old Religion from wood and natural objects. 14 Weston Road, Strood, Kent ME2 3EZ.

SORCERER'S APPRENTICE, 4/8 Burley Lodge Road, Leeds LS6 1QP. Rare herbs, oils, scents, incenses, temple requisites.

QUEST, edited by Marian Green since 1970, is published each quarter and deals with all aspects of modern magic. There is also an Annual Conference in London each March and the *Quest* team runs postal courses on Ritual Magic, Aquarian Magic and others on Natural

Magic/Witchcraft. *Quest* also arranges local meetings of the Green Circle, an open study group, with occasional weekend or one day courses on magic, healing, etc.

AQUARIAN PRESS publishes new and classic books on magic, astrology, self-development, mysticism and esoteric thought. Full catalogue sent on request: Denington Estate, Wellingborough, Northamptonshire NN8 2RQ.

There are a number of Festivals each year all over Great Britain concerned with health, psychic development, self-awareness and meditation. Further information will be found in the national press or in the relevant magazines.

INDEX